Introduction

This booklet covers all the law you need for Unit 2B AQA law. This is the civil part of Concepts of Liability. It includes the civil law of the tort of negligence together with the procedure for bringing a claim to court and the assessment of compensation, called damages.

In order to be able to claim compensation for harm caused by D's negligence, three things must be proved:

The defendant (D) owes the claimant (C) a duty of care

D breached that duty

D's breach caused the harm to C

These three taken together show D has been negligent. Negligence is a tort, which in French means 'wrong'. For our purposes, tort is a wrong done to a person who can then claim compensation from the wrongdoer by taking the case to court.

The court procedure has already been covered in Unit 1 but here it is specific to a civil claim in negligence and you may have to apply it briefly to a given situation. The final thing to consider in any civil claim is the assessment of damages as monetary compensation for the harm caused.

There is a chapter on each of the three parts to the tort of negligence, and a chapter on the procedure for bringing a claim and assessing compensation for the wrong done. A revision chapter then highlights the main points of these four chapters with more tasks, and the final chapter is examination practice.

The tasks are intended to reinforce your learning so do these as you go along. There are plenty of tasks to help with explaining and applying the law. The answers are at the end of the booklet.

Examination tip

There are rules for helping the courts to decide on each of the three matters which prove negligence. It is important to know these rules with at least a case example on each.

Task 1

Create a document (either in a notebook or on screen) to note down the main rules with a case on each as you read though the law in this book. The key cases are highlighted, these are the 'must know' ones but you will need others to help you recognise how a particular situation may be dealt with in court. The more cases you are aware of the better equipped you will be when it comes to exam time.

"You must take reasonable care to avoid acts or omissions which you can reasonably foresee would be likely to injure your neighbour" – Lord Atkin

Establishing a duty of care is based on what is known as the 'neighbour principle' or 'neighbour test' from **Donoghue v Stevenson 1932**. This case is famous for establishing liability in negligence, and is often referred to as 'the snail in the ginger beer case'.

Key case

Mrs Donoghue was in a café with her friend. She drank some ginger beer with her ice cream, and later she emptied the rest of the contents into a glass. To her horror, a decomposing snail came out. She was ill (whether from drinking the beer or from seeing the snail in its state of decomposition is not clear) and sued the manufacturer. As her friend had paid, there was an important legal issue to consider. Mrs Donoghue was owed no duty under contract law because she did not buy the drink herself. The case eventually went to the HL on the issue of whether the manufacturer could owe a duty in tort to a consumer who did not buy the goods. This was new ground. Until this case, only those with a contract could sue if harm was caused by a product. The HL decided that the relationship between a manufacturer of a product and a consumer of that product was sufficiently close to warrant imposing a duty on the manufacturer to take care that a consumer is not harmed by the product. So a precedent was set and tort law now protects those without a contract. The closeness of the relationship is an important factor in proving duty and became known as the 'neighbour principle' after the leading judgment in the case.

The neighbour principle

Lord Atkin gave the leading judgment in **Donoghue v Stevenson** and produced the now famous 'neighbour principle'. He said that the biblical requirement that we must 'love our neighbour' became, in law, that we must not injure our neighbour. He said, *"You must take reasonable care to avoid acts or omissions which you can reasonably foresee would be likely to injure your neighbour"*. He then goes on to answer the question 'who then, in law, is my neighbour?' and answers, *"persons who are so closely and directly affected by my act that I ought reasonably to have them in contemplation as being so affected when I am directing my mind to the acts or omissions which are called in question"*

Example

I am baby-sitting for someone at work and being paid. I have a contract so I owe a duty under the contract, and can be sued if the baby is harmed due to my negligence. However, if I am baby-sitting for free, perhaps for a friend, then there is no contract. Since **Donoghue v Stevenson**, I can be sued in tort, as I owe a duty to anyone affected by my acts or omissions. The baby would be someone I would have in mind when I am contemplating, or thinking about, doing, (or omitting to do), whatever is being questioned – my negligent action (or inaction).

In **Grant v Australian Knitting Mills 1935**, a man had bought some underpants and contracted a skin disease due to a chemical in the material. In deciding the manufacturer owed him a duty of care the court followed the case of **Donoghue v Stevenson**. A person (the consumer) wearing a manufacturer's products (in this case the underpants) is someone likely to be *closely and directly affected* by the manufacturer's actions (producing the underpants). The manufacturer, therefore, ought *reasonably to have them in contemplation* when making the product, so the consumer satisfies the 'neighbour' test and the manufacturer owes them a duty of care.

The test is essentially one of foreseeability. If the result of your actions may foreseeably harm someone, you will owe that someone a duty of care.

Task 1

You may not be able to remember the neighbour principle in full so write out Lord Atkin's statement and then put it in your own words so it is clear to you.

In **Caparo v Dickman 1990**, the HL said that there was no general principle which applied to all cases and it was necessary to consider whether imposing a duty was 'just and reasonable' in the circumstances. A three-part test was established to expand on the neighbour test.

The Caparo test

For a duty to arise:

there must be foreseeability of harm

there must be proximity between C and D

it must be fair, just and reasonable to impose a duty on D

Key case

In **Caparo v Dickman**, C had claimed that the auditors of a company's books owed him a duty of care. They had produced inaccurate accounts and he had lost money by investing in the company. Arguably, it was foreseeable that people in his position, who had relied on the accounts, would suffer loss. The HL held, however, that there was insufficient proximity between him and the auditors. The auditors produced the accounts for the company, to comply with the legal requirements to produce annual accounts, not for potential investors. Nor was it fair, just and reasonable to make the auditors liable for losses to unknown investors.

The first two parts of the **Caparo** test are similar to the neighbour test from **Donoghue v Stevenson**. The third is a matter of what is fair in the circumstances of the particular case and allows for a certain amount of flexibility, based on what is 'fair' in the particular situation.

In brief:

Caparo	Donoghue	Meaning
it must be foreseeable that someone will be harmed by D's actions	D should have that someone 'in contemplation' when acting	'someone' is a group, or class, of people not an individual. Thus a duty was owed to all consumers, not to Mrs Donoghue in particular. It is foreseeable that a consumer will be affected by the act or omission of a manufacturer.
there is proximity between C & D	C is D's 'neighbour'	there is some kind of legal connection or relationship between C & D
it is fair, just and reasonable to impose a duty on D	Not specifically mentioned, although it was arguably the attempt to achieve justice that extended the law	A matter of policy, of what is right in the circumstances

Taking each in turn, let us expand a little and also see how the law is applied.

Foreseeability

It must be foreseeable that D's act (or omission) could cause harm.

Example

In **Donoghue v Stevenson**, it was foreseeable that the manufacturer's act (of allowing a snail to get in the bottle), or omission, (the failure to clean the bottles properly), could harm a consumer of the ginger beer.

We covered foreseeability earlier when looking at the neighbour principle and it is the same under **Caparo v Dickman**. Although note that despite Lord Atkin's words in **Donoghue v Stevenson** that you should avoid acts or omissions which *"you"* can foresee might injure your neighbour; the test for foreseeability is an objective one. This means it is what the *reasonable person* foresees, not what D foresees.

Example

In **Kent v Griffiths 2000**, a doctor called an ambulance for a woman who had an asthma attack. Despite only being a few miles away, it took nearly 40 minutes to arrive and she suffered respiratory arrest. The ambulance service argued that there was no duty of care. The CA held that it was reasonably foreseeable that a person could suffer further harm as a result of a delay and there was no good reason for the delay. A duty was owed.

Task 2

Read the **Donoghue v Stevenson** case and answer the following questions.

Why couldn't Mrs Donoghue sue the shopkeeper?

Whom did she sue and what did the HL decide?

Why was this case important?

What is the neighbour principle?

Proximity

The concepts of foreseeability and proximity overlap. The more proximate (closer) you are to someone, the more foreseeable it is that his or her actions may harm you. In **Bourhill v Young 1943**, a woman heard a motorcycle crash and went to the scene after the rider's body had been taken away. She saw blood on the road and claimed that the shock caused her to miscarry and lose her baby. She failed in her claim against the negligent driver, as she hadn't actually seen the accident. It was not *foreseeable* that she would be harmed nor was she in close *proximity* to the driver or the accident. A passenger would be affected by a driver's actions so would be owed a duty of care. A pedestrian near to where someone is driving could also be affected and so be owed a duty, but a women who was not in the vicinity would not be foreseeably affected by the driver's actions so there is no duty. It is not just physical proximity however (called proximity in time and space because it means being at the scene at the time of the event), but whether the *relationship* between the parties is proximate enough. This is similar to the neighbour principle under **Donoghue v Stevenson**, where it was said a neighbour was someone closely affected by another's actions. Although in the driving example that is usually someone in physical proximity, in the case of a manufacturer it can be purely a matter of relationship.

Examples

In **Donoghue v Stevenson**, the relationship was one between a manufacturer and consumers. In **Caparo v Dickman**, there was proximity of relationship between the auditors and the company whose accounts they did, but not between the auditors and investors. The latter relationship was not sufficiently close, or 'proximate'.

In **Kent v Griffiths** above, in deciding there was a duty of care, the CA also noted that the ambulance service was in sufficiently close proximity to a patient once it had accepted the call and sent an ambulance to collect that patient.

Fair, just and reasonable to impose a duty

This is a matter of public policy and is perhaps the most difficult of the three parts of the Caparo test. It means that the court looks at what is best for society as a whole and / or may restrict the duty to avoid 'opening the floodgates' to claims. The latter situation can be seen in **Caparo v Dickman** itself, where the accounts would be available to the public so anyone might see them and rely on them. This could open the floodgates to an infinite number of claims, so it would not be fair to impose a duty in this situation. Actions against public bodies such as the police, hospitals, rescue services and local councils may also fail on this part of the test because these groups provide a public service (which is good for society) paid for from public funds (which would be seriously depleted if too many claims were made). This means that the courts may refuse to impose a duty on such groups, even though harm is foreseeable.

Key case

In **Hill v CC for West Yorkshire 1988**, a consequence of the 'Yorkshire ripper' case, the police were held not to owe a duty to potential victims of a crime after releasing a suspected killer through lack of evidence. When he killed again the mother of the victim sued the police, claiming they owed a duty to her daughter. The HL refused to find a duty, partly on lack of proximity between the police and an unknown member of the public. However, the policy issue also arose. The HL felt that the threat of being sued could make the police less efficient in carrying out their duties. This would not be in the public interest so it was not 'fair, just and reasonable' to impose a duty.

Immunity for the police is not, however, absolute. There have been several successful claims against the police where there has been a greater degree of proximity. This shows that all three parts of the test are connected. The more foreseeable something is, and the greater the degree of proximity, the more likely it is that it will be fair, just and reasonable to impose a duty. In **Reeves v MPC 1999**, the police were held to owe a duty to a prisoner who committed suicide whilst in their care and whom they knew to be a suicide risk. The police had left the door flap open and he used it to hang himself. An important factor in **Reeves** was that the police *knew* that he was a suicide risk. In another suicide case, **Orange v CC of West Yorkshire Police 2001**, a similar claim failed. In this case, the man who hanged himself while in custody, after being arrested whilst drunk, was *not* a known suicide risk.

Examples

Reeves v MPC can be used to illustrate all three parts of the test. Harm was *foreseeable* because the police knew that he was a suicide risk. There was *proximity* between C and the police because he was in one of the police cells. In such circumstances, it seems *fair, just and reasonable* to impose a duty on the police to the group of people – prisoners – who are in their care. There were no policy reasons to exclude a duty as it was to a limited, and known, group of people so would not make policing generally inefficient. Also, imposing a duty in these circumstances would not lead to a flood of claims as the duty would only be to prisoners in police care who were foreseeably at risk of harm.

Kent v Griffiths can also be used to illustrate all three parts of the test. We saw above that there was foreseeability of harm because of the delay, and there was proximity between an ambulance service and the person it was sent to collect. In deciding there was a duty of care, the CA also considered this last factor and held that where no good reason for a delay is given it is fair, just and reasonable that an ambulance service should owe a duty of care as regards the promptness of the pickup of a patient. This case distinguished cases against the police such as **Hill v CC for West Yorkshire** as here there was a specific patient who would be affected by the delay, not the public in general.

Local councils also have some immunity from owing a duty of care. In **Fernquest v Swansea CC 2011**, a man sued the council after slipping on ice at a bus stop. The judge applied **Caparo v Dickman** and held that there was proximity between the council who ran the bus service and people using the service. In addition, the risk of injury was foreseeable because the council knew about the ice. On appeal, the CA reversed the decision based on the third part of the test. The CA held that although injury was foreseeable, it was not fair, just and reasonable to impose a duty of care on a council for 'normal hazards' which members of the public could be expected to be aware of.

So you can see that, as with the police, immunity is not absolute. The three parts of the test overlap to some extent, the higher the risk of harm (foreseeability) and the closer the relationship (proximity) the more likely a duty will be owed.

In **Vernon Knight Associates v Cornwall CC 2013**, the CA held that a council owed a duty to local residents to keep drains clear to prevent flooding. It was therefore liable when it failed to do so. The council knew the risk of flooding during times of heavy rainfall and had previously taken steps to keep the drains clear. Flooding was highly foreseeable and there is a close relationship between a council and local residents. It was therefore fair, just and reasonable to impose a duty of care on the council which they had breached by not keeping the drains clear on this occasion.

Sporting activities and certain types of entertainment are seen as for the public benefit so the courts may feel it is not 'fair, just and reasonable' to impose a duty on the people providing for such events. However, much depends on the circumstances and again the more foreseeable harm is, and the closer the relationship, the more likely it will be fair to impose a duty. In **Watson v British Boxing Board 2000**, the boxer Michael Watson suffered head injuries during a fight against Chris Eubank. He sued the Board on the basis that had proper medical treatment been given at the ringside he would not have suffered brain damage. The CA found that it was 'just and reasonable' to impose a duty on the Board to ensure adequate medical facilities were available, and upheld his claim. A similar decision was made in **Vowles v Evans 2003**, where a player was injured in an amateur rugby match when a scrum collapsed. Without going into the finer details of the rules of rugby, the essence was that the scrum collapsed due to the referee not applying the rules properly, and the player sued. Recognising that the rapport between referee and players is crucial to a good game of rugby, the court held that this would not be lessened by the knowledge that the referee owed a duty of care for the players' safety. Applying **Caparo v Dickman**, the CA held that as a matter of policy it is 'just and reasonable' that the law should impose a duty to take reasonable care for the players' safety. This could be achieved by the sensible and appropriate application of the laws of the game. **Vowles** can be compared to **Hill**, where it was thought police efficiency *would* be lessened by imposing a duty of care.

Task 3

The last two cases were based on whether imposing a duty was fair, just and reasonable. However, this is only one part of the test. Apply the other two parts of the test to **Watson v British Boxing Board** and **Vowles v Evans**.

Omissions

In **Donoghue v Stevenson**, Lord Atkin referred to *"acts or omissions"*. This means D can be liable for *not* doing something, as well as doing something negligently. Liability for an omission occurs when there is a particularly close relationship, such as that between an employer and employee. There will also be liability where there is a high degree of control by one person over another; there will be a duty to take care of that person's safety and failure to do so may result in liability. An example is omitting to take care to prevent the man's suicide in **Reeves v MPC**.

Where there is a risk of harm and that risk was created, or known about, by D there is a duty to take steps to avoid it harming anyone and omitting to do so can result in liability. This is true even if the danger has actually been created by a third party, but only if D knew of it.

In **Smith v Littlewoods 1987**, an owner of a disused cinema had left his property unsecured and vandals broke in. They caused a fire which spread to a neighbour's property. The omission here was not locking up the disused building properly. The neighbour sued the cinema owner on the basis that this omission had caused the fire damage. The claim failed because the owner had no idea that vandals had broken in so harm was not foreseeable. However, had the owner known of the vandals he would have been obliged to take action to prevent harm to others. The claim also failed on the issue of causation (D successfully argued that the act of the vandals had broken the chain of causation between the omission to secure the building and the fire) but the case illustrates the point that it is possible to have liability for an omission as well for an act.

You can see from this case that the issue of omissions connects with foreseeability. If D had known of the vandals breaking into the cinema then the damage would be more foreseeable and so a greater obligation to take care would arise. However the court made clear that a property owner is not expected to put a 24-hour guard on a property to ensure nobody enters it and creates a risk of damage to neighbouring property.

Examination tip

The courts have made clear that the **Caparo** test is only important to *novel* categories of negligence. This means that you should only need to use the 3-part test where it is a new situation and has not been in court before. An examiner may use a scenario where there is a clear duty because you are expected to focus on another issue, like breach or causation. However, it is possible the examiner wants to check that you understand how the test applies, so if you are not sure the best thing to do is to apply the **Caparo** test briefly and then move on to the other issues.

Example

It has already been established, in **Donoghue v Stevenson**, that a manufacturer owes a duty to a consumer so this is not a 'novel' situation. If you have a scenario involving a manufacturer and consumer you can use **Donoghue** to say briefly that there will be a duty and then move on to breach or causation. If you are not sure (or the examiner specifically asks you to apply the test) then say it is foreseeable that a consumer will be affected by a manufacturer's actions and there is proximity between them as established in **Donoghue**. It is also fair, just and reasonable to impose a duty as it is only to a limited group of people (those consuming that manufacturer's products) and there are no policy reasons to exclude it.

Task 4

Franny is driving too fast because she is late for college. As she rounds a corner she sees a child in the road and slams on her brakes. Her passenger and the child are both injured. Outline the principles of a duty of care and explain whether Franny owes either the passenger or the child a duty.

Summary

Donoghue v Stevenson – the neighbour test on foreseeability

Caparo v Dickman – the 3-part test

Foreseeability (the likelihood of D's actions causing harm to C/whether a reasonable person would foresee it)

Proximity (a relationship between D & C – the parties to the action)

Whether it is fair, just and reasonable to impose a duty. (Based on what is good for society and whether there should be immunity for, e.g., the police or a local council, and also whether imposing a duty of care will open the floodgates to other claims)

Terminology

Make sure you understand the following terms:

Tort – a civil wrong

C – an abbreviation for the claimant

D - an abbreviation for the defendant

Duty of care – a duty owed by D to C

Foreseeability – whether a reasonable person would foresee harm

Proximity – closeness in space, time or relationship between C & D

Fair, just and reasonable – a matter of policy and whether there is a reason not to impose a duty on D

Self-test Questions on duty

*What is the 3-part **Caparo** test?*

*Why was there no duty in **Bourhill v Young**?*

*Why was no duty owed in **Caparo v Dickman**?*

Who might be immune from owing a duty?

*Why was a duty owed in **Fernquest v Swansea CC** but not in Vernon Knight Associates v Cornwall CC?*

For a range of free interactive exercises please go to **www.drsr.org** and click on 'Free Exercises' to see what's available.

"We must not look at the 1947 accident with 1954 spectacles" – Denning LJ

A breach of duty occurs when D has not taken sufficient care, i.e., has been negligent. To decide this, an objective test is used. The courts will consider what a reasonable person would have done given the same circumstances. In **Blyth v Birmingham Waterworks Co. 1856**, Baron Alderson said:

"Negligence is the omission to do something which a reasonable man ... would do, or doing something which a prudent and reasonable man would not do."

Who is the 'reasonable man'?

Firstly, we would now say 'reasonable person'. When deciding if D is in breach of duty the court will consider what a reasonable person would have done in similar circumstances to D. Although this is objective, in that it is not what D did but what a reasonable person would do that matters, the reasonable person is someone that is supposedly in D's position.

Examples

We saw in **Vowles v Evans 2002**, that a referee in an amateur rugby match owed a duty of care for the players' safety. By allowing an inexperienced player to play in a scrum position for which he was not trained the referee was in breach of his duty. He hadn't reached the standard expected of a reasonable person in those circumstances, i.e., *a reasonable referee*.

In **Harris v Perry 2008**, a couple hired a bouncy castle for a birthday party and a boy was seriously injured by another child while playing on it. The judge held the couple had breached their duty of care by not supervising the children at all times. There was a higher risk of harm because children of different ages, and sizes, were playing together. The CA reversed the decision and held the standard of care required was that of a *reasonably careful parent*. In the circumstances, a reasonably careful parent would have acted in the same way so they had reached the required standard. The CA noted that it was impossible to avoid all risk that children might injure themselves or each other when playing together.

In **Daw v Intel Corp (UK) Ltd 2007**, an employer knew an employee was suffering from severe stress but did little to remedy the situation. The CA upheld the decision that help had not been adequately provided so the employer had not reached the standard expected of a *reasonable employer* and was in breach of duty. The CA also restated the factors which apply in establishing breach and said an employer is only in breach of duty if there is a failure to take the steps which are reasonable in the circumstances, bearing in mind the magnitude of the risk of harm occurring, the gravity of the harm which may occur, the costs and practicability of preventing it, and the justifications for taking the risk.

There are slightly different rules in the cases of children and professionals, and we will look at these after considering how the courts decide how a reasonable person would have acted. There are no 'key' cases for breach as the courts will balance several factors in deciding what is reasonable. Different cases illustrate each point.

The factors for establishing breach

As was restated by the CA in **Daw v Intel Corp (UK) Ltd**, there are four main factors which are taken into account when deciding what a reasonable person would do. These have the effect of lowering or raising the standard expected and they are usually referred to as:

the magnitude of risk

the gravity of the potential harm

whether the risk was justifiable

the expense and practicality of taking precautions

Make sure you understand how each of the factors apply, and learn at least one case on each. The more cases you know, the easier it is to see what is needed when considering an examination scenario. The factors are balanced against each other in deciding whether D has done what is reasonable in the circumstances.

The magnitude of risk (or the degree of risk i.e., how likely is it that harm may occur?)

This factor raises the standard expected if the degree of risk is high. The greater the risk of harm, the greater is the obligation on D to take precautions. On the other hand, no breach will have occurred if the risk was impossible to foresee.

Example

In **Fardon v Harcourt-Rivington 1932**, D's car was parked on a street with a dog inside. As C walked past the dog jumped up and broke the window and some glass went in C's eye. There was no breach because the risk was impossible to foresee. The HL held there was no duty to guard against "fantastic possibilities".

In **Roe v Ministry of Health 1954**, contamination of an anaesthetic left C paralysed. Medical knowledge at the time was not such that this could have been expected; in fact it was this event that alerted the medical profession to the problem. There was no known, or foreseeable, risk, so the Ministry of Health was not liable. The court will not use hindsight to assess this. In **Roe**, Denning LJ made the comment opening this section on breach. It is whether the risk of harm was foreseeable *at the time*. Similarly in **Williams v University of Birmingham 2011**, a physics student who had been exposed to low levels of asbestos over 30 years before he became ill, sued the University. The CA held that the lack of knowledge of the dangers of exposure to small amounts of asbestos at the time meant the University had not breached its duty.

This shows that where the magnitude of risk is low there is unlikely to be a breach. In **Blair-Ford v CRS Adventures Ltd 2012**, C took part in a 'welly-wanging' contest at an activity centre. He was throwing a wellington boot backwards between his legs when he overbalanced and broke his neck. He sued for compensation. The judge ruled that it was a freak and tragic accident and rejected his claim.

In **Uren v Corporate Leisure 2013**, a man who was injured during a game at an RAF base sued the organisers of the game and the Ministry of Defence in negligence. The game involved running to an inflatable pool and then getting over the side to retrieve a piece of fruit floating in the water. C dived in head first and broke his neck. He argued that as the water was shallow going in head-first should have been prohibited. At trial, the court found that although there was some risk of harm from such an activity it was very small, and the existence of such a small risk along with the fact there was some social value to outdoor activities, meant there was no breach of duty. This seems similar to **Blair-Ford v CRS Adventures Ltd**. However after an appeal, a retrial was ordered and the decision was reversed. This time the court said the harm was more than minimally foreseeable and D should have taken precautions to avoid it.

If the risk is foreseeable, but small, the other factors may be relevant in deciding whether D had done enough. In **Bolton v Stone 1951**, a woman was hit by a cricket ball whilst walking near a cricket ground. The cricket club had taken precautions by erecting a 17-foot fence and the ball had gone over it only a matter of 5or 6 times in some 35 years. There was thus a foreseeable, but only very small, risk of a ball going over and, balanced against the other factors, the club had done all that was expected of it.

Task 5

Explain what Lord Denning meant when he said *"We must not look at the 1947 accident with 1954 spectacles"*. Which case did he say this in and to which factor is it most relevant?

the gravity of the potential harm (how serious is the harm that could occur?)

This factor also raises the standard expected where the harm is likely to be serious. A higher standard of care may be required where, although the *risk* is small, the *consequences* may be serious. This can be seen in **Paris v Stepney BC 1951**, where C was a worker who was already blind in one eye. Whilst doing some welding he was injured in the other eye. His job only involved a slight risk of injury, but the HL held that although a failure to provide goggles would not always make the council liable to their employees, in this case the seriousness of the harm that *could* occur was very great, because he was already blind in one eye. There was therefore a duty to take greater care. This shows that a particular characteristic of the victim could raise the standard expected. The council knew he was blind in one eye so should have taken greater care to protect him from harm.

Examination tip

The **Paris** case shows that a greater duty is owed to those suffering under a disability. This could also apply to children or the elderly, so look for clues in the scenario. What may be doing enough in respect of a fully able person may not be so in other cases. Note also that it is *potential* harm that is looked at. Don't be tempted to say that there is a breach because the harm actually suffered is very great. It is what harm *might* occur that is relevant, not what *has* occurred. This was confirmed in **Daw v Intel Corp (UK) Ltd**, where the CA referred to the gravity of the harm "which *may* occur".

whether the risk was justifiable (is there a good reason for taking the risk?)

The taking of a risk may be justifiable in certain circumstances, and if so the standard expected is lower. A risk which is of some benefit to society, for example, may be deemed acceptable even though it could be foreseen. In **Watt v Hertfordshire CC 1954**, a fireman was injured when a heavy car jack fell on him. The vehicle he was in was not adapted to carry such equipment, but it was held that this was an acceptable risk in the circumstances because they were on their way to rescue a woman trapped under a car.

Many sports and games have a social benefit which may make a risk of harm justifiable. However, risk-taking for the sake of it will not be acceptable even where there is a social benefit.

In **The Scout Association v Mark Barnes 2010**, the CA considered several breach factors in assessing whether the Association had breached its duty of care by allowing a game to be played with minimal lighting. The game involved running around and grabbing an object in the dark. The main lights were off but the emergency lighting was on and therefore there was some light. When a boy collided with a bench he injured his shoulder and sued. The trial judge found the Association had breached its duty of care and they appealed. On appeal the CA held that, balancing the risk of injury, the foreseeability of harm, the cost of preventing harm and the social benefit of the activity, there was a breach. The CA said that it was not the function of the law of tort to eliminate all risks but that the social value was limited and excitement for the sake of it did not justify the risk of harm.

Note also the **Compensation Act 2006 s 1**. This provides that in deciding whether D should have taken particular steps to meet the standard of care (e.g., take precautions) a court may consider whether a requirement to take those steps might prevent a desirable activity from being undertaken or discourage people from undertaking functions in connection with a desirable activity. This means a risk of harm may be justifiable when the activity in question is desirable, such as school trips and sporting events.

the expense and practicality of taking precautions (how much would it cost to avoid the risk and is it realistic to expect precautions to be taken to avoid it?)

D may argue that avoiding a risk altogether would be too costly. The courts are unlikely to accept risk-taking based *solely* on the cost of avoidance, but it may tip the balance when considering the other factors. In **Latimer v AEC 1952**, the HL found a factory owner not liable for the injury to an employee who slipped on a wet floor. It was wet due to exceptional rain and flooding, and the owners had put down sand and taken other precautions. On the facts they had done enough. Shutting the factory would not only have been costly, but also impractical.

Examples

If everyone drove at 5 m.p.h. there would be fewer road accidents, but no one would expect the government to rule that such precautions should be taken. That would be impractical. In **Bolton v Stone**, the cricket club had already built a high fence – arguably, it would be impractical to do more than they had done, as in **Latimer**. By comparison, in **Paris v Stepney BC**, it would have been neither costly nor impractical to provide goggles.

Taking precautions by driving more slowly may, however, be deemed reasonable in certain circumstances. In **Belka v Prosperini 2011**, C had drunk about four pints of beer and he and a friend were crossing a dual carriageway near a roundabout. C ran across the second carriageway, leaving his friend on the middle section. He was hit by a taxi and claimed in negligence for his injuries. The taxi driver had said in evidence that he saw the friend in the middle section, but did not see C. The court found that he had breached his duty by not slowing down after seeing the friend. Had he done so (i.e., taken precautions) the accident could have been avoided.

Harris v Perry 2008 illustrates several factors. There was a high risk of harm because children of different ages, and sizes, were playing together. However, in considering what precautions should reasonably have been taken to protect against the risk of harm the CA held that it was impractical for parents to keep children under constant surveillance or supervision and it was impossible to avoid all risk that children might injure themselves or each other when playing together. Finally, the CA held that it would not be in the public interest to impose a duty upon them to do take further precautions against any risk of harm. In deciding they were not in breach the CA referred to the incident as "*a freak and tragic accident*".

In **Uren v Corporate Leisure 2013**, discussed above, the court held that even though the risk was small and there was some social benefit, more precautions should have been taken, such as banning diving head-first. This can be compared to **Bolton v Stone**, where sufficient precautions were taken. It also illustrates how the factors are balanced against each other.

Examination tip

It is important to understand that these factors are balanced against each other and no particular factor will lead to a finding of breach alone. Look for particular clues in the given scenario so that you pick the relevant factors and the most appropriate case to use in support of your arguments. It may be that you need to discuss all four if the facts indicate all may be relevant.

Task 6

Using **Bolton v Stone**, apply all four factors to assess whether the cricket club acted reasonably.

Objectiveness, children and professionals

The standard expected is said to be objective. It is based on what the reasonable person would do. A striking illustration of this is **Nettleship v Weston 1971**. Here a learner driver was liable for injuries to her driving instructor due to her negligent driving. The CA said that a learner driver should show the skill of an ordinary, competent driver.

However, the standard is also measured by reference to the particular circumstances. Thus, it is the standard expected of a reasonable parent, employer etc., as we saw earlier. This makes it slightly more subjective. In particular, the standard is modified a little in the case of children (of whom a lower standard is expected) and professionals (of whom a higher standard is expected). A child would be expected to reach the standard of a child of similar age, not an adult.

Example

In **Mullin v Richards 1998**, a schoolgirl of 15 was injured during a play-fight with another girl, using plastic rulers as swords. The CA found the other girl not to be liable in negligence. The point here was that although an adult may have seen the risk, a child would not.

In **Orchard v Lee 2009**, two boys had injured a playground supervisor whilst playing tag. Both were 13-years-old and the judge followed **Mullin v Richards** and held that the test was whether a 'prudent and reasonable' 13-year-old would have expected any injury to occur from his actions. The CA agreed and held that the primary question was whether their conduct had fallen below the standard that should objectively be expected of a reasonable child of that age. In the circumstance, they had been playing in an authorised play area and not breaking any rules. This was a simple accident and there was no liability in negligence.

In **Palmer v Cornwall CC 2009**, a claim was brought in respect of another incident which occurred during play-time at a school. A boy of 14 hit another boy in the eye while throwing stones at seagulls. The play area was supervised by dinner ladies and at the time only one was on duty. The victim's claim was rejected at trial but the CA reversed the decision and held that only one supervisor for around 300 children was clearly inadequate. If better supervision had been provided the boys may not have been throwing stones because they knew this was against the school rules. This time the claim succeeded, but this may be because it was brought against the council and not the other boy. Had the claim been against the other boy it may well have failed on the basis of **Mullin**, or as in **Orchard v Lee**.

Where D acts in a professional capacity the standard expected is that of a person in that line of work. This is often seen in cases of medical negligence, although it applies to all professions. In medical cases the courts consider what is known as the '**Bolam** principle' established in **Bolam v Friern HMC 1957** and modified by the case of **Bolitho v City & Hackney HA**. This principle is used to assess whether errors of judgment by a doctor should be actionable in tort.

In **Bolam v Friern HMC**, it was accepted that if a doctor acted in accordance with 'a practice accepted as proper by a reasonable body of medical men' there would be no breach and therefore no liability.

Example

A doctor is examining a patient and fails to notice an abnormality which later leads to the patient developing cancer. Whether this error of judgment is a breach of the doctor's duty of care to the patient will depend on whether other doctors would have taken more care. If the doctor acted in the same way as other doctors would have done, this will be seen as acting in accordance with 'a practice accepted as proper by a reasonable body of medical men' and the doctor will not be in breach.

The **Bolam** principle was modified slightly in **Bolitho v City & Hackney HA 1998**, where the HL added that the medical opinion must have some logical basis. Thus a doctor must show the skill that would be normal practice according to reasonable medical opinion, i.e., what a reasonable body of medical men (and women) would expect of a doctor, not just any 'reasonable person'. Additionally, that medical opinion must have a logical basis.

In **Bolitho v City & Hackney HA**, a doctor failed to attend promptly to a patient and the patient subsequently died from a blocked airway. The doctor argued that even if she had attended she would not have intubated the patient. The HL confirmed the **Bolam** test but held that if the medical opinion was not capable of withstanding logical analysis the judge would be entitled to hold it was not reasonable or responsible. On the facts of the case, although there was conflicting medical evidence, the HL held that her action was supported by a responsible body of medical opinion which was not illogical. Both **Bolam v Friern HMC** and **Bolitho v City & Hackney HA** were followed in **R v Royal National Orthopaedic Hospital NHS Trust 2012**, where the court held that in most cases the fact that distinguished experts in the field were of a particular opinion would demonstrate that the opinion was reasonable. However, the court also held that in rare cases, if the opinion was incapable of withstanding logical analysis judges were entitled not to use it to assess the standard of care expected. The idea is that the court does not want C to produce some kind of 'expert' witness to say "I would have done just the same" if this is not what would be normal procedure.

A further point, made by the court in **Wilsher v Essex AHA**, is that although a junior doctor would be expected to show the standard of a qualified doctor (which accords with the principle in **Nettleship** that D is judged against a 'normal, competent person'), the post the doctor is in will be relevant, so that the standard expected of a junior doctor will be less than that expected of a consultant.

Examination tip

Although these are medical cases the same principle will apply to other professions. If your examination scenario involves a professional person then you can use these cases to support an answer that says that the person will be judged against what is accepted practice in the opinions of others in that particular profession, as long as there is a logical basis for that opinion. If the person concerned is a learner or trainee you may also need to discuss **Nettleship v Weston**. An example seen in an examination paper was that of a trainee hairdresser, where you would be expected to explain that a trainee hairdresser should show the standard of care expected of a competent hairdresser (**Nettleship**) and that the standard will be judged against the opinion of other responsible hairdressers (**Bolam**) and this opinion must have a logical basis (**Bolitho v City & Hackney HA**).

Note that the 'balancing factors' are still relevant in cases where there is a subjective element such as age or professional competence. In **McDonnell v Holwerda 2005**, the question was whether a general practitioner (GP) had fallen below the standard expected of a reasonably competent GP by not recognising the possibility of meningitis in a child, following an examination. The court held that she had not fallen below the standard expected on the first occasion that she assessed the child. However, the GP had seen the child on a second occasion and, as the degree of risk was high due to the fact that the meningitis infection spreads so quickly, and the potential harm could be serious as meningitis can kill, the standard expected was higher. She had fallen below this standard because she had not carried out a full enough investigation, i.e., she had not taken reasonable precautions against the risk.

There are plenty of other cases on breach. For more examples look back at the 'duty' cases. In **Vernon Knight Associates v Cornwall CC 2013**, the council had not reached the standard expected of a reasonable council because there was a known risk of flooding and they had failed to take precautions against that risk by keeping the drains clear. They were therefore in breach of their duty to local residents. In **Vowles v Evans**, the referee had not reached the expected standard of a referee so had breached his duty to the players.

Task 7

Remember that in order to even consider breach there must first be a duty, so any case you see where breach is an issue will be an example of someone owing someone else a duty even if no breach was proved. Look back at the facts of the following cases on breach of duty and state who owed a duty to whom. The first is done for you as an example.

Bolton v Stone – the cricket club owed a duty to passers-by

Paris v Stepney BC

Watt v Hertfordshire CC

Latimer v AEC

Nettleship v Weston

Mullin v Richards

Bolam v Friern HMC

McDonnell v Holwerda

Vowles v Evans

Examination tip

It is clear from the cases that the standard expected will always depend on the particular circumstances. Look carefully at the facts of a scenario for clues, e.g., mention of D's profession or age. Then apply the factors as appropriate, e.g., mention of something happening often indicates a high degree of risk, mention of a social activity indicates the risk may be justifiable. Balance the relevant factors as the court would do and conclude whether D is likely to be in breach of duty.

Task 8

Choose any 3 cases seen so far and consider which factors may have been relevant in deciding whether there was breach of a duty of care. See how many of them you can apply, as you did with **Bolton v Stone** for Task 6.

Summary

Breach is based on the standard of the reasonable person. The circumstances are relevant so D will be compared to a reasonable person in the same circumstances, e.g.:

Reasonable parent

Reasonable employer

Reasonable child

Reasonable doctor

What is deemed reasonable is based on 4 factors:

The magnitude or degree of risk

The gravity or seriousness of potential harm

Whether the risk was justifiable

The expense and practicality of taking precautions

Task 9

Draw up the summary into a diagram, adding a case on each, and keep it for revision.

Make sure you understand the following terms:

Standard of care – the expected level of care to be decided by balancing several factors

Breach of duty – not reaching the expected standard of care

Foreseeability – whether some harm is foreseeable, the more foreseeable the harm the more likely there is a breach of duty

Objective – relating to a reasonable person

Subjective – relating to a particular person

Self-test Questions on breach

In which case was the objective standard explained, and by whom?

What standard is expected of a professional?

What standard is expected of a child?

*Why had the employer breached their duty in **Daw v Intel Corp (UK) Ltd?***

For a range of free interactive exercises please go to **www.drsr.org** and click on 'Free Exercises' to see what's available.

"... children's ingenuity in finding unexpected ways of doing mischief to themselves and others should never be underestimated" – Lord Hoffmann

The third matter that must be proved before D is liable is causation. C not only has to prove that damage occurred, but must also prove D's act or omission was the cause of that damage, both in fact and in law. Damage must be factually caused by D's breach and be reasonably foreseeable.

Causation in fact

The question here is whether D's breach in fact caused the damage. The courts apply the 'but for' test. This asks, "'but for' D's negligence would the harm have occurred?" If the answer is "no" then D is liable. However, if the damage would have happened regardless of the negligent act or omission, D will not be liable for it.

Example

Using an earlier case, **Paris v Stepney BC**, we can see that 'but for' the employer's breach of duty (not making sure the employee wore goggles) the employee would not have been injured in the eye. The breach therefore factually caused the harm. Had the worker been injured in the arm then wearing goggles would not have prevented this. In that case we would say that 'but for' the breach the employee would still have been injured, so the breach did not factually cause the harm.

Key case

The leading case is **Barnett v Chelsea & Kensington HMC 1968**. A man suffering from vomiting and pain called at a hospital, but he was sent home without being treated. He later died of arsenic poisoning and his widow sued the hospital management committee. The hospital clearly owed a duty to patients, and was found to be in breach of this duty as the man was not even given an examination. However, they were not liable in negligence because he would have died regardless of whether he was treated. Here the answer to "But for D's negligence would the harm have occurred?" was "Yes, it would", so D was not liable. Both duty and breach were proved, but the claim failed on the 3rd issue – that of causation.

In **Bolitho v City & Hackney HA**, discussed with breach of duty, the doctor had argued that the patient would have died even if she had attended promptly. The HL confirmed that the **Bolam** test applied to causation as well as breach and that, as there was a logical body of medical opinion that would not have taken the particular action to save the patient (intubation of the airway), it could not be said that her lack of doing so caused his death. It is likely that, as in **Barnett**, he would have died anyway.

In **Dalling v R J Heale & Co 2011**, C had suffered injuries while drunk and claimed these were causally related to an earlier head injury which had impaired his ability to control his drinking. He had successfully sued D for the first incident but D now argued that the second injury was caused by C's voluntary drinking and not by the earlier injury. The court held that 'but for' the original head injury C would not have suffered the second injury because the first incident contributed to his lack of control, and also the harm was foreseeable and not too remote (see causation in law below). The evidence showed that C rarely drank to excess before the incident. D was liable.

In **Sutton v Syston RFC 2011**, a rugby player was injured when he fell on a sharp object hidden in the grass. He sued the club arguing that had a pre-match inspection of the pitch been carried out he would not have been injured. The CA held that although an inspection should be carried out before a match, this would not have revealed the object which was nearly completely hidden. The breach (not inspecting the pitch) did not cause the harm.

Successive and multiple causes

In cases where there is more than one possible cause of harm, a claim could fail if causation could not be proved in respect of any particular D. This is because if there is more than one breach, the 'but for' test can be hard to satisfy.

Example

Carl works for two employers both of whom have been negligent and exposed him to chemicals. He becomes sick and has to take several months off work. He wants to claim in negligence for the harm caused. The problem for Carl is that he cannot prove which exposure caused the sickness so cannot say but for one particular employer's negligence the disease would not have occurred.

This problem can occur where breaches follow after each other (successive causes) and where there is more than one breach and any one of them could have been the possible cause (multiple causes, as in my example), and in such cases the rules have been modified.

The court in **Performance Cars Ltd v Abraham 1962**, held that in most cases of successive causes the original person in breach will be liable. Thus C could not claim from a later negligent driver for repairs to his car previously damaged in a similar accident by another driver. It was the original driver who had caused the damage (which had not yet been repaired).

Multiple causes are treated slightly differently and the rule from the case of **Fairchild** is used. In **Fairchild v Glenhaven Funeral Services Ltd 2002**, the HL made it clear that the 'but for' test is *necessary* but not always *conclusive*, and modified the rules.

Key case

The facts of **Fairchild** were that C became ill after exposure to asbestos dust in the course of successive employments. The CA had held that he could not recover damages from any of the employers, since he could not establish which period of employment had caused his illness. This seemed unfair to C, because each of the employers could be shown to be in breach of duty. It just wasn't clear which particular breach was the cause of the illness. The HL reversed the CA's decision and held that if C could show that D had '*materially increased the risk*' of harm then the causation test could be satisfied. The HL said that the causation rules might be modified on policy grounds '*in special circumstances*'.

In **Barker v Corus UK Ltd 2006**, with similar facts, the HL developed the rule in **Fairchild v Glenhaven Funeral Services Ltd** and held that the **Fairchild** exception to the 'but for' test could apply when there is more than one possible cause of harm, even if these include causes which would not usually lead to an action in tort (in this case a period of self-employment). However, damages would be apportioned according to how far each D had materially increased the risk of injury rather than any one D being liable in full.

The idea of apportioning damages between different Ds as established in **Barker** was reversed by an amendment to the **Compensation Act 2006**, which provides in **s 3** that in mesothelioma (a type of cancer) cases each person who contributes to the harm can be liable in full. However the Act only applies to mesothelioma cases so **Barker** will still be good law for other types of claim.

In **Bailey v Ministry of Defence and another 2008**, hospital negligence and an infection had led to a woman becoming weak. She later had other treatment elsewhere and suffered brain damage. The later treatment was not negligent so she sued the first hospital. The hospital argued it was not only their negligence that made her weak, but also the infection, and that a contribution to the risk of injury was not enough to prove causation. The judge disagreed, the correct question was whether the negligence had 'caused or materially contributed to' the injury, and it had. The CA upheld the decision and held that as long as D's act made a material contribution to the harm, causation could be proved, even if there was another, non-negligent, cause which also made a material contribution.

These are complicated rules so let's sum up.

The basic test comes from **Barnett v Chelsea & Kensington HMC** and provides that if the harm would not have occurred 'but for' D's breach, factual causation is proved.

Fairchild modifies the rule where there are several possible breaches, so that even if C cannot say 'but for' a particular D's breach the injury would not have occurred, causation will still be proved if any one D materially increased the risk of harm. Anyone who contributed in this way can be liable for the full damages.

Barker adds that where there are several possible causes, including non-negligent ones, damages can be apportioned between any Ds whose breach materially contributed to the risk of harm, in accordance with that contribution.

The **Compensation Act** provides that C can claim the total damages from any one D who contributes to the risk of harm rather than apportion them between the Ds. However, this only applies in mesothelioma cases.

Even if duty and breach is proved, and also that D's act was the factual cause of the harm, there is still one more hurdle for C to surmount. The harm must not be 'too remote' from D's breach of duty.

Task 10

Choose a case from the previous chapter on breach and apply the 'but for' test to see if the breach caused the harm.

Causation in law: Remoteness of Damage

The test here is one of reasonable foreseeability. If the loss or damage is not reasonably foreseeable it is said to be 'too remote' from the breach. This was established in **The Wagon Mound 1961**, which replaced the wider test in **Re Polemis 1921**, that you were liable for *all* the direct consequences of your negligent actions.

Example

Your teacher negligently spills coffee over you and you have to change your clothes. This makes you late leaving college and by this time a storm has started. As you cycle home your bike is struck by lightning and you are injured. It can be said that 'but for' your teacher spilling coffee you would not have been delayed and so would not have been struck by lightning and injured. However the lightning is not foreseeable so is too remote from the breach. Causation in law is therefore not proved.

The full name of **The Wagon Mound** is **Overseas Tankship (UK) Ltd v Morts Dock & Engineering Co 1961**, but it is commonly called **The Wagon Mound**. The test from this case is that D is only liable for the foreseeable consequences of any breach of duty. If a reasonable person would foresee the result of the breach then D is liable. If not then causation in law is not proved and D is not liable.

Key case

In **The Wagon Mound**, oil was negligently spilt by the Ds from their ship. This oil caused a fire that damaged C's wharf two days later. The Ds were not liable because it was not believed that this type of oil could catch fire on water. The damage to the wharf by *oil* was foreseeable, so C could claim for this, but not damage caused by the later *fire*. That damage was too 'remote' from D's act, because it was not foreseeable.

Intervening act

Sometimes something happens between D's negligent act and C's injury. This is referred to by the Latin tag *'novus actus interveniens'* or in modern parlance, 'new act intervening'. Such an act may sometimes break the chain of causation between D's act or omission and the harm to C. In **Smith v Littlewoods 1987**, an owner of a disused cinema had left his property unsecured and vandals broke in. They caused a fire which spread to a neighbour's property. The neighbour sued the cinema owner. The claim failed. D successfully argued that the act of the vandals had broken the chain between the omission (not locking up properly) and the damage. An example of the argument failing can be seen in a case we looked at earlier, **Reeves v MPC**. The police argued that the prisoner's suicide was an intervening act, which broke the chain of causation. The HL did not accept this as it was foreseeable (the police knew he was a suicide risk).

In **Corr v IBC Vehicles Ltd 2008**, a widow had claimed damages in respect of her husband's suicide six years after he had an accident at work. The issue was whether the suicide was foreseeable, i.e., whether the breach had *caused* the suicide or whether it was too *remote*. The trial court found that the suicide was not foreseeable and that, based on **The Wagon Mound**, foreseeability was an essential requirement of establishing both duty and damage caused. The CA reversed this decision and restated that as long as the type of harm was foreseeable the particular outcome need not be. The HL upheld the CA's decision. Several issues arose, but the main ones concerned causation, specifically foreseeability and breaking the chain. The HL held that severe depression was foreseeable and as it was of a similar type to depression there was no need for suicide itself to be foreseeable. The suicide did not break the chain of causation as it was not a conscious voluntary act, but a response to his depression.

Overlap

Note the overlap between foreseeability and intervening act. An intervening act will only break the chain of causation if it was unforeseeable itself.

In **Reeves v MPC**, the prisoner was on suicide watch so suicide was foreseeable and didn't break the chain. If the police had left the door flap open and a mouse had crawled in through the hole and then bitten the prisoner who happened to suffer a rare allergy to mouse bites and died, this would be an unforeseeable event and so would be likely to break the chain between the negligence of the police and the death.

Type of damage

If the *type* of damage is foreseeable, then the fact that it occurred in an unforeseeable way, or that the consequences were more extensive than could be foreseen, will not affect liability. In **Hughes v Lord Advocate 1963**, a child knocked over a paraffin lamp which caused an explosion. He was very badly burnt. The court found that the *type* of injury was foreseeable (burns) even though the way this had occurred (an explosion) was not. D was liable.

The principles of both **The Wagon Mound** and **Hughes** were confirmed by the HL in **Jolley v Sutton LBC 2000**.

Key case

In **Jolley**, a 14-year old boy was badly injured when working with a friend on an abandoned and derelict boat on council land. The CA had held that the council were not liable. Whilst it may be foreseeable that children might *play* on such a boat it was not foreseeable that they would attempt to *repair* it. The HL reversed the decision and made the point in the opening quote that the ingenuity of children should not be underestimated. It was foreseeable that they would meddle with the boat in some way – it did not matter that they had been repairing it rather than playing on it.

In **Hadlow v Peterborough CC 2011**, a teacher was working at a secure unit for young women who could be prone to violence. She should have had a member of the unit's care staff with her during lessons. When she noticed that the staff who escorted the three women to the lesson had both left and locked the door behind them, she jumped up to call out to them before they were out of earshot. In her hurry she tripped and injured herself. The issue to be decided was one of causation. It was accepted that had one of the women attacked her the unit would have been liable, as they were in breach of duty by not ensuring she had someone with her. However, the unit argued that their breach did not cause the harm because she had not been attacked – she injured herself by tripping over her chair. The CA, following **Hughes**, held that as the type of injury was foreseeable (the breach of duty had exposed the teacher to the risk of harm) even though it happened in an unforeseeable way (her attempt to remove the risk by getting the attention of the staff), the unit was liable.

The principle in **Hughes** extends the remoteness test from the **The Wagon Mound**. The harm itself does not necessarily have to be foreseeable, as long as that type of harm was. It would appear that the wider principle is correct because it was approved by the HL in **Jolley** and seen again in **Hadlow**.

It may be important to refer to **Jolley**, not just **The Wagon Mound** test, if the scenario involves children. Use **The Wagon Mound** as setting the test, but go on to mention the point made in **Jolley** that the ingenuity of children should not be underestimated. This could mean that something that would not be foreseeable where adults were concerned, and so would fail the test for legal causation under the **Wagon Mound**, would be foreseeable in the case of a child, who can be expected to do the unexpected.

Use two cases that you remember from looking at duty or breach. Use the 'but for' test to apply causation *in fact*. Then add the rules from **The Wagon Mound** and **Jolley** to see if D *legally* caused the harm.

The thin skull rule

There is another apparent exception to the foreseeability test. It is a common law rule that D must take the victim as he or she is found. This means that if a particular disability in the victim means they are likely to suffer more serious harm, or die, D is still liable, even though a person without that disability would not have been so seriously harmed. An example is **Smith v Leech Brain 1962**, where D's negligence caused a small burn, which activated a latent cancer from which C died. His wife sued his employer and the court held that C's particular vulnerability (the pre-existing cancer) did not affect liability. C's wife did not have to prove that cancer was foreseeable, only that some harm was, even though it was of a different type. It is called the 'thin' or 'egg shell' skull rule because the essence of the rule is that if there is something which makes V more vulnerable than other people this will not affect D's liability.

Jake is riding his bike too fast and knocks over a man who has a very thin skull. Most people would have only suffered a few knocks and bruises, but this man dies because as he fell his skull broke. Jake can be liable for the death, not just the foreseeable injuries, under the 'thin skull' rule.

Summary

When applying the law ask the following questions.

> **Would the harm have occurred 'but for' D's act or omission?**
>
> **Was the harm foreseeable or was it too remote?**
>
> **Was this type of harm foreseeable?**
>
> **Does the thin-skull rule apply?**

Apply the law on duty, breach and causation to the facts of **Barnett v Kensington & Chelsea HMC**.

Make sure you understand the following terms:

The 'but for' test – whether the result would have happened 'but for' D's breach of duty

Successive causes – a second or third possible cause of C's harm that follows from an earlier breach

Multiple causes – several possible causes of C's harm

Mesothelioma – a type of cancer

Causation in law – a link between D's actions and C's harm

Remoteness of damage – where the result of the harm is too far (remote) from the breach so D is not liable

Foreseeability – the type of harm must be foreseeable, if not it is too remote so D is not liable

Intervening act – something that happens after D's breach, which can break the chain of causation if it is not foreseeable

The thin-skull rule - D must take the victim as he or she is found including any vulnerability or pre-existing illness

Self-test questions on causation

What is the 'but for' test and from which case did it come?

Which case established the rule on foreseeability?

*What did **Hughes** add to this?*

Can you explain the 'thin-skull rule'?

*What was the point made in **Jolley** (in the HL) in regard to children?*

For a range of free interactive exercises please go to **www.drsr.org** and click on 'Free Exercises' to see what's available.

As mentioned earlier, the court procedure has been covered in Unit 1. Here we look at it again in so far as it applies to a civil claim in negligence. Then we will look at how the courts assess the compensation which is paid if the claim succeeds.

Bringing a claim – the procedure

As you have studied the courts for Unit 1, this part will be by way of revision of the main points as they apply in a negligence claim. As you know the 'Woolf Reforms' in 1999 made significant changes to the way cases are dealt with. Since then, further changes have been made to the Civil Procedure Rules 1998 regarding the maximum amounts which can be claimed in a small claim or on the fast track in the county court.

The very first step when making a claim is to negotiate. Negotiation takes place between the parties and if no agreement is reached then one or both may go to a solicitor. The solicitor will still try to negotiate and a letter before action from C's solicitor is the next step. This sets out what will be in the claim should it go to court and is an attempt to reach a settlement at this stage without the need for a court case. The cost and time involved often means people feel it is not worthwhile taking a case to court. This is why the reforms were needed, to simplify procedures and reduce both time and costs. Another part of this pre-action protocol is that both parties must let the other side see all relevant documents. This is called 'disclosure'. These steps leading up to a court case are called 'pre-action protocol' and the aim is to avoid court if possible. Negotiations tend to go on right up until the case itself, often resulting in a settlement 'on the doorstep' of the court. This means a claim is started while negotiations continue. All actions which go to court must start with the issue of a claim form and D has 14 days to respond to this. If the claim is ignored, C can ask the court to make a judgment in default. If the claim is defended both parties must fill in a directions questionnaire. The two relevant courts for a civil claim are the county court and the High Court. Which court a case is heard in is decided by both the amount of the claim and the complexity of the case. The directions questionnaire will help the judge decide on this. There are three different tracks which cases may be allocated to.

The first track is the **small claims track** and cases on this track are heard in a special room in the county court. The maximum claim for this track is £10,000, and in personal injury cases it is £1,000. A district judge presides over the case which is heard in private rather than the usual open court.   Parties are encouraged to represent themselves and to reach an agreement, and the case is less adversarial than those in open court where solicitors usually act for each party to argue their client's case.

The next track is the **fast track** and this deals with claims between £10,000 and £25,000. Cases on this track will start in the county court, again with a district judge. There is a strict time-table set by the judge so that the case is dealt with speedily and efficiently (within 30 weeks). Costs are also limited so people have a better idea of what their 'day in court' is going to cost.

The third track is the **multi-track** and all cases over £25,000 are allocated to this track. Cases on this track will start in the High Court. Again the judge will manage the case and set a time-table, sometimes following a case management meeting.

Although cases on the fast track start in the county court and cases on the multi-track start in the High Court there is a provision in the Civil Procedure Rules for the case to be moved up a track if it is very complex or down a track if it is relatively simple. This means some simple cases can be heard in the county court even if the amount involved is quite high. Similarly a complex case involving a relatively small amount of money may be heard in the High Court.

Claim up to £10,000
- Small claims track
- County court
- In private

£10-£25,000
- Fast track
- County court (possible move to High Court if complex)
- In open court

Over £25,000
- Multi-track
- High Court (possible move to county court if simple)
- In open court

The main point with the reforms is that cases are dealt with as quickly and efficiently as possible.

Whichever court is used, the judge will usually encourage the parties to consider some form of alternative dispute resolution (ADR) in an effort to avoid high costs and prolonged trials. ADR has become more important since the reforms as alternatives to the court system are specifically encouraged. The reduction in legal aid in many cases has further led to an increased use of ADR. One form of ADR is negotiation and as we saw above this is the normal first step and may be directly between the parties to the action or between their solicitors. It is quite informal and there is no fixed procedure involved, just discussions between the two sides to attempt a compromise. Many cases will be automatically referred to mediation, which is similar but involves a third party so is a little more formal. There is talk of making mediation in small claims cases compulsory but at the moment (April 2015) this only happens if the parties agree, although it is a free service provided by the court. Where mediation is used an impartial counsellor or specialist in the area under dispute will meet with the two parties and help them to come to a mutually-agreeable solution to the problem. Other than for a small claim this service has to be paid for by the parties. Often the parties to the dispute never meet but put their views to the mediator separately. This has the effect of keeping the discussions calm and the mediator will pass on any offer or counter-offer to the other party. Mediation will frequently result in a compromise that is acceptable to both parties. There are other types of ADR which you will have seen in Unit 1 but these mostly apply to employment or commercial situations so are not repeated here.

If ADR fails to produce an agreement then the case will proceed to court and be managed by a judge, as discussed above.

Task 13

Go to the Citizen's Advice site and see what they say about bringing a claim. The home page is at http://www.adviceguide.org.uk/england.htm. Then search for 'civil claim' and follow the various links on the rules, going to court, what to do before bringing a claim etc. There is a step-by-step guide to the procedure and a range of information about bringing a claim (and currently the site is more up-to-date than the government one). There are also some useful sheets on ADR which can be downloaded as PDF documents. These links sometimes don't work correctly so just use the one above which goes to the home page and type ADR into the search box.

Summary

Before looking at how compensation is assessed, there are two other matters you need to know about bringing a civil claim. These are the burden of proof and the standard of proof.

The burden of proof and the standard of proof

The burden of proof means who bears the burden of proving the case. In civil cases the burden is on the claimant. The claimant must provide evidence of the wrongdoing (for our purposes this is the tort of negligence and requires proof of duty, breach and causation). The standard of proof means how much has to be proved. In criminal law, the standard is very high (beyond reasonable doubt) but in civil law it is lower and is called the 'balance of probabilities'. This is anything over 50% so if there was a 51% probability that D was in breach of duty this will be enough.

There is a special rule for a claim in negligence called *res ipsa loquitur*. This is Latin and means 'the thing speaks for itself'. For the rule to apply the 'thing' must be under D's control and be the cause of the harm, if so then C need not prove breach of duty. Although it effectively seems to reverse the burden of proof, at least in part, it is still up to C to prove that the rule applies. However, where it does apply there is no need for C to find evidence to prove negligence because by the nature of the event negligence must have occurred, i.e., the thing speaks for itself. It is then up to D to prove there was no negligence.

Example

Sandi goes to hospital for an operation to remove her appendix. A few days after the operation she has bad stomach pains. Eventually an X-Ray is taken and this shows that a metal clip has been left in her stomach. On these facts there is obvious negligence; the clip could not have got there by itself so the surgeon who took out her appendix must have left it there. The surgeon was clearly in control of the operation and the instruments used, so will therefore be seen as negligent using *res ipsa loquitur* – the thing speaks for itself.

Key case

The main case on the rule is **Scott v London and St Katherine Docks 1865** where some sacks of sugar fell from a crane at the docks and injured a passer-by. The court held that for the rule to apply, as well as showing that the thing which caused the harm was under D's control, C must show that the harm could not have been caused except by negligence and that there was no clear reason for the accident, i.e., the exact cause is unknown so it would be hard for C to prove. Here it was not clear what had caused the bags to fall but the crane was under the control of the dock company and it could only have happened by negligence of some kind, so the rule applied.

Another example is **Ward v Tesco Stores 1976**. Here a customer slipped on some spilt yoghurt in the supermarket. It was not clear how the yoghurt got there but it should not have been left for a customer to slip on. The court held the doctrine of *res ipsa loquitur* applied and that Tesco was liable.

The issue of control is important and two similar cases help to illustrate this. In **Gee v Metropolitan Railway 1873**, a child was injured when a train door came open just after the train left the station. The railway company was seen to be in control of the door at this time so *res ipsa loquitur* applied. In **Easson v LNER 1944**, a child was again injured when a train door came open but this time the train was several miles from the station and the court held that the railway company were no longer in control of the door (someone else could have opened it and not closed it properly) so the rule did not apply.

Task 14

Explain what is meant by the following terms

Burden of proof

Standard of proof

Res ipsa loquitur

Damages: Compensation for the harm caused

The most usual remedy in tort is an award of damages. This is intended to compensate the claimant rather than punish the defendant. The aim is to return the claimant, as far as this is possible, to the position he or she would have been in if the tort had not occurred. Damages are only claimable in respect of foreseeable loss; this is as for causation and based on **The Wagon Mound** test for remoteness of damage.

Examination tip

Be careful not to confuse 'damage' with 'damages'. Although both relate to foreseeability of harm the term damage relates to the actual loss, the harm or damage to property caused by D. The expression 'damages' is a term used for the monetary award, the compensation to C. Read the question carefully to make sure you are answering it correctly.

The amount awarded by the court may be a once and for all payment, i.e., the full amount is paid as a lump sum, or by way of a structured settlement, where an annuity is taken out and the compensation paid as regular instalments. These are most commonly used for the larger awards and / or long-term loss, e.g., where C is unable to work again.

There are two types of damages, called special and general damages. Apart from loss of future earnings the first is quantifiable and is included in the claim. The second, plus any loss of future earnings, is assessed by the court.

Special damages

Special damages include loss of earnings and expenses paid out because of the harm or damage caused. They cover all losses from the time of the breach of duty to the date of the trial. These are reasonably straightforward and can usually be agreed between the parties. They are easy to quantify as pay slips and receipts can be produced to cover loss of earnings and things like damage to a car or other belongings, transport costs, medical expenses etc.

Loss of future earnings is calculated by taking the current earnings and multiplying it by a figure (called the multiplier) representing the number of likely working years but reduced to account for investment income and the possibility of reduced employment for other reasons. No allowance is made for inflation or tax. The multiplier is usually a maximum of 18 years but in certain employment situations may be less, as in **Collett v Smith 2008**. In this case a footballer injured his leg while playing for Manchester United reserve team at age 18. He retired a few years later because of the injury. The court had to decide whether he would have succeeded in making a career in professional football and, if so, at what level and for how long. There was evidence that he would have gone on to play at Championship and Premiership level. He was awarded nearly four million pounds based on the lost chance of a successful career, with the multiplier set at 11 years. This would have taken him to the normal age for a footballer retiring of 35 years.

Loss of earnings capacity may be awarded if the harm caused has meant C has less chance of getting a job. In **Smith v Manchester Corporation 1974**, C was injured and because she then had a reduced chance of getting further employment an award was made in respect of this.

Damages are further classified as *pecuniary* or *non-pecuniary*. Pecuniary loss means financial loss so pecuniary damages are things like expenses and loss of earnings as discussed above. Thus, pecuniary loss comes within special damages. Non-pecuniary loss is any loss which does not have a quantifiable monetary value. It therefore has to be assessed by the court. It includes compensation for the injury itself, distress, pain and suffering and loss of amenity. These all come within general damages discussed below.

General damages

General damages cover pain and suffering, loss of amenity and the injury itself. The court will assess this by reference to other recent cases and information supplied by the Judicial Studies Board. No award for pain is awarded if the claimant is unconscious or cannot feel pain. Distress at disfigurement, reduced life expectancy etc. may be included in suffering. Loss of amenity relates to quality of life. This is also based on conventional sums, provided by the Judicial Studies Board, but may be increased if the injury affected a special interest or hobby.

Example

My hobby is cycling and due to someone's negligence I am badly injured. I have to have a leg amputated. In addition to any claim for compensation for loss of earnings and expenses, I can claim for the *pain and suffering* caused by the injury and a set amount for the *injury itself*, the loss of a leg. I can claim a further amount to compensate me for not being able to carry on with my hobby – this would come under *loss of amenity*.

Examination tip

If you are asked to discuss damages in relation to a particular scenario you should look carefully for clues to see whether loss of amenity may be applicable. Reference to, e.g., C being a keen cyclist would indicate that if the injury prevented cycling then an extra amount would be awarded for loss of amenity to compensate for this, as in my example.

Most social security benefits are deductible from the award. Private insurance, charity, gifts etc. are not deductible.

The final point on damages is that C is expected to minimise or 'mitigate' any loss. D is not expected to pay compensation for any harm or damage that could have been avoided by C taking reasonable steps.

Example

Clare's hand is injured in an accident caused by Dan's negligence. She refuses to get medical treatment and an infection spreads into her arm which has to be amputated. Can she claim for the amputation or only the injury to her hand? We can say that it is reasonable for Clare to seek medical help for the first injury and therefore it is not reasonable to make D pay for the amputation. This further injury was easily preventable as seeking medical attention should not be difficult. However, if it is not reasonable to expect Clare to mitigate her loss by getting medical help, say because she lived on a remote island and she could not find transport to a hospital, then Dan will be expected to pay in full for the amputation and any associated pain and suffering or loss of amenity.

Summary

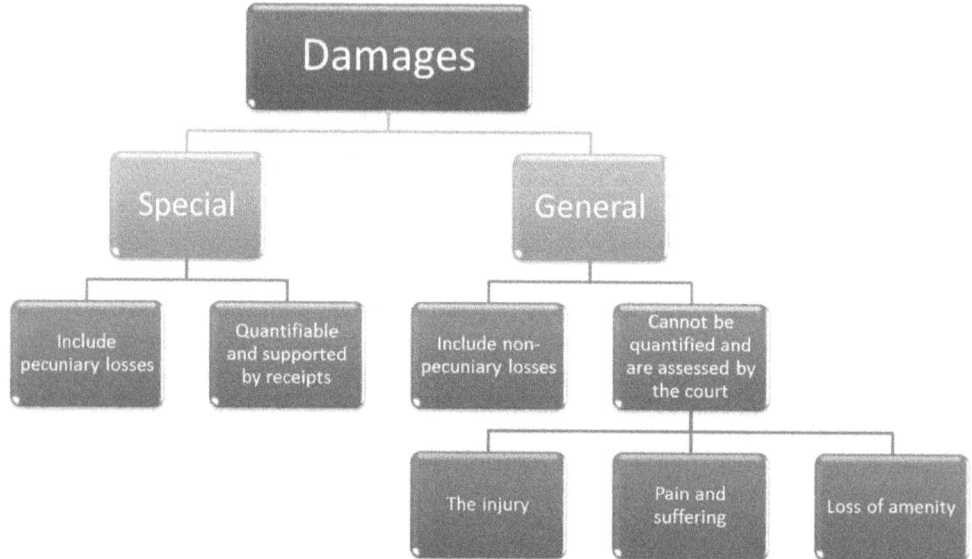

Terminology

There are not many cases to learn, but a lot of new terms come into this area. Make sure you understand the following:

Negotiation – a discussion between the parties (or their solicitors) in an attempt to reach a settlement and avoid a court case

Letter before action – a letter from C's solicitor setting out what will be in the claim should it go to court (also in an attempt to reach a settlement)

Disclosure - letting the other side see all relevant documents

Alternative dispute resolution (ADR) – various other ways to settle a dispute without going to court

Mediation – a type of ADR where an impartial counsellor or specialist meets both parties and helps them reach a solution

Pre-action protocol – all the steps prior to the court action

Small claims track – for claims up to £10,000

Fast track – for claims up to £25,000

Multi- track – for claims over £25,000

The burden of proof – who has to prove the case in court. In civil cases the burden is on the claimant

The standard of proof – how much has to be proved. In civil law it is the 'balance of probabilities'

Res ipsa loquitur – a Latin phrase which means 'the thing speaks for itself'

Damages – an amount of money intended to compensate the claimant

Special damages – loss of earnings and expenses to the date of the trial

The multiplier – a figure representing the number of C's likely working years

Pecuniary damages –financial loss

Non-pecuniary damages – losses other than financial ones

Loss of amenity – something which relates to C's quality of life, such as a hobby or special interest

General damages – non-pecuniary losses such as pain and suffering and loss of amenity which must be assessed by the court

Self-test questions

What is a small claim?

In which court is a small claim heard?

What is the maximum sum under the fast-track system?

Why might a fast-track case be transferred to the High Court?

What is the difference between special and general damages?

What does pecuniary loss mean?

For a range of free interactive exercises please go to **www.drsr.org** and click on 'Free Exercises' to see what's available.

Chapter 5: Revision

A general guide to revision

The first and foremost rule for revision is to start early. Too many students leave it until the last minute and then get in a panic. If you take it gently and organise your time properly you will feel a lot more calm and confident when exam time comes. Make a plan of what you want to cover each day and try to stick to it. Don't forget to include some breaks in your schedule. If you are tired it will be harder to retain the material you have been revising.

Here are a few tips for revision techniques

Go through your notes and try to summarise them

Learn the key cases, as these are essential to know

Make sure you understand how the judge has applied the law to the facts so you can do the same in an examination scenario

Go through the summaries of the topic. These provide the essential points which may need to be addressed

Go to the examination board's website for past exam papers, mark schemes and reports

Practise answering questions then look at the examiners' mark schemes and reports to see if you were on the right track

Revision of this Unit

Proving a duty of care is the first step in any negligence claim. Harm must be foreseeable, so consider whether D's actions are likely to cause harm to a person in C's position, e.g., a manufacturer's actions could harm a consumer, a doctor's actions could harm a patient etc. There must be proximity between C and D. This includes not only physical proximity but also the *relationship* between the parties, as with the manufacturer-consumer and doctor-patient examples above. In **Bourhill v Young**, she did not have sufficient proximity to the accident (no physical proximity) or to the driver (no relationship) so the claimed failed. In **Donoghue v Stevenson** the relationship between a manufacture and consumer was sufficiently close so the claim succeeded.

Task 15

Briefly explain why the claim succeeded in **Reeves v MPC** but failed in **Orange v CC of West Yorkshire Police** in similar circumstances.

The fair, just and reasonable part of the test is more difficult because it is based on what is fair in the circumstances so decisions of the courts sometimes seem to conflict.

Examination tip

Make sure you know a few cases on the third part of the test, so you can support an answer to a particular given scenario. It is useful to know a case where the decision differed from another with similar facts as it gives you a chance to support an answer either way if you are not sure.

Task 16

Find two other cases on the third part of the test where the decision differed and explain why this was.

Breach of duty

The standard expected of D is that of the reasonable person, an objective test. Note, though the subjective element:

Bolam v Friern HMC/Bolitho v City & Hackney HA – the medical profession and other professionals

Nettleship v Weston – learners

Mullin v Richards – children

There are four main factors to balance against each other in deciding what is reasonable:

the **magnitude or degree of risk** – how likely is it that harm will occur? **Bolton v Stone**

the **gravity or seriousness of the potential harm** – how much harm might occur? **Paris v Stepney BC 1951**

whether the **risk was justifiable** – is the risk of harm a benefit to society in some way? **Watt v Hertfordshire CC 1954**

the **expense and practicality of taking precautions** – how easy is it to avoid the harm occurring? **Latimer v AEC 1952**

Summary

Breach of duty

The courts will consider:

The degree of risk

The seriousness of potential harm

Whether the risk was justifiable

The expense and practicality of taking precautions

These factors are balanced against each other when the courts are deciding whether D breached the standard of care to be expected

Where D acts in a professional capacity, the skill expected is that of the profession – **Bolam / Bolitho**

Task 17: Case study

In **Gibson v Chief Constable of Strathclyde Police 1999**, a bridge collapsed and was in a dangerous state. A police officer took charge of the scene but then left it unattended without putting up cones, barriers or other signs. A passing motorist was injured by the bridge further collapsing. He sued the police claiming they had been negligent.

Explain and apply the test from **Caparo v Dickman** to these facts to decide if a duty of care was owed.

Now apply the rules on breach of duty to decide if the police have breached any duty that might be owed.

Damage caused by the breach

Causation must be proved both in fact and in law. If D's act or omission did not cause the harm there is no liability. This means considering the following questions:

> Would the harm have occurred 'but for' D's act or omission? **Barnett v Chelsea & Kensington HMC**

> Was the harm foreseeable or was it too remote? **The Wagon Mound**

> Was this type of harm foreseeable? **Hughes v Lord Advocate**

> Does the thin-skull rule apply? **Smith v Leech Brain**

Task 18

Apply the rules on causation to the facts of **Gibson v Chief Constable of Strathclyde Police** in Task 17

Summary

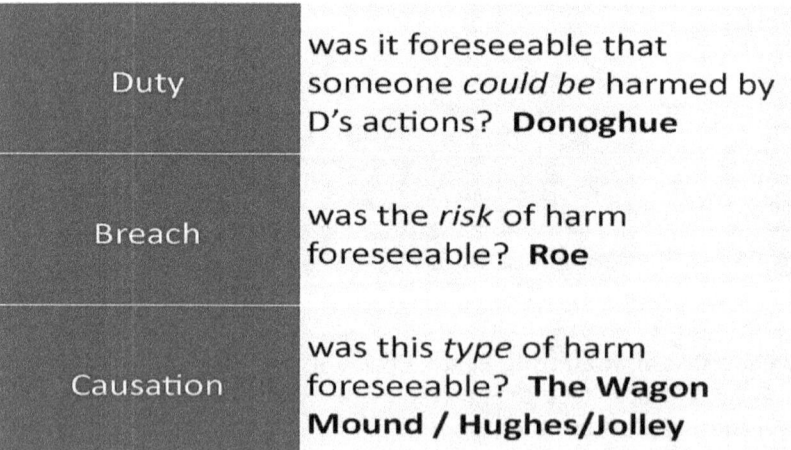

Note that foreseeability comes into all 3 areas, but becomes more specific at each stage.

Duty	was it foreseeable that someone *could be* harmed by D's actions? **Donoghue**
Breach	was the *risk* of harm foreseeable? **Roe**
Causation	was this *type* of harm foreseeable? **The Wagon Mound / Hughes/Jolley**

Once negligence has been proved then the next thing to consider is going to court and getting compensation for the harm done.

The courts

The two civil courts in which a claim for negligence may be brought are the county court and the High Court.

38

The three tracks which govern where a claim will start are the small claims track, the fast track and the multi-track.

Task 19

Briefly explain the three tracks.

Alternatives to the courts

Negotiation is the first step in any claim and may be directly between the parties to the action or between their solicitors. If the negotiations succeed then the courts may be avoided altogether. However, if negotiations fail then the case will go to court.

Once a case goes to court the judge will encourage the parties to consider some form of alternative dispute resolution (ADR). One form of ADR is mediation. This is similar to negotiation but involves a third party (the mediator) so is a little more formal. Many cases will be automatically referred to mediation if the parties agree.

Damages

The amount awarded by the court may be a once and for all payment or by way of a structured settlement, paid in instalments. Structured settlements are used for larger claims where C is unable to work again.

Damages are divided into special and general and pecuniary and non-pecuniary.

Special damages are quantifiable and included in the claim along with receipts.

General damages cannot be quantified and are assessed by the court. They include:

The injury itself

Pain and suffering

Loss of amenity

Pecuniary means financial so comes within special damages. Non-pecuniary losses will be those which come under general damages as they cannot be quantified in monetary terms but must be assessed by the courts.

Finally, C is expected to take reasonable steps to mitigate the loss.

Task 20

Tariq drives into Pam's car which is parked outside her house. His passenger Dave is badly injured and likely to be off work for several months. Pam's car is damaged and will cost £500 to repair. Briefly explain the purpose of damages and how and where the two claims by Dave and Pam will be dealt with.

For a range of free interactive exercises please go to **www.drsr.org** and click on 'Free Exercises' to see what's available.

A brief general guide

This is a test of law so you need to state the legal principles involved and apply them to the particular scenario. A small plan may be helpful.

It is necessary to do more than regurgitate your notes. You need to be selective as to what is relevant, and to choose appropriate cases and examples in support of what you say. This means you should never put in irrelevant material just because you know it. The examiner wants to know that you understand the specific issues and can apply the appropriate law to the facts given.

Always support your answer with **relevant** cases. Don't worry too much about the facts, the principle forming the *ratio decidendi* is usually the important part, For example, in **Donoghue v Stevenson** the principle that you owe a duty to people affected by your actions is the important part, you don't need to write a paragraph discussing snails and ginger beer.

Having said that, you want to show why you have chosen a particular case so will need to mention any facts that specifically relate to the scenario. If the scenario mentions someone being ill after consuming a chocolate bar with a dead mouse in it (yes, there has been a case!) then talking briefly about snails in ginger beer will be relevant. The main point here is that you need to be selective; this demonstrates a skill in itself and also conserves precious time.

If you can't remember the name of a case that is relevant, don't leave it out but refer to it in a general way e.g. 'in one decided case ...', 'in the case where there was a snail in a drink' or 'in a similar case ...'

Examination tip

When you apply the law refer to the facts of the scenario as you go along. Failure to do this is a common complaint seen in examiners' reports. Referring to the specific facts not only shows the examiner that you are answering the particular issues raised by the scenario, but also stops you drifting off the point.

Finally, make sure you cover the whole question; there are only a certain number of marks available. The examiner has a mark scheme to work to, so however brilliant your answer to one part of the question is, missing out another part will reduce your total marks. The paper is 90 minutes long and the marks are 45 plus 2 for A03 for each scenario (including the compulsory criminal scenario). This means that you should spend no more than 1 minute for each mark, i.e., for an 8 mark question aim at spending no more than 8 minutes.

Applying the law

Application of the law requires you to be selective. The facts should point you to particular issues which need addressing and you must be prepared to pick out the relevant law and cases and to leave out anything irrelevant – for which you will gain no marks. An examination scenario is often based on an actual case so try to learn plenty of these as this will help you see what is needed. The more cases you know the easier it is for you to recognise how the law might deal with a particular situation.

To practice 'clue-spotting' do the following exercise.

Task 21: Application practice – clue-spotting

Look at the comments taken from problem scenarios and add what they indicate is the focus of the question as regards proving a breach of duty. The scenario is not fully explained as this is an exercise to encourage you to look for clues rather than answer a full question; however in each case you can assume someone has suffered harm. The first is done for you (in italics) as an example.

Jenny was a trainee hairdresser and made a mistake when mixing the hair dye. *This indicates the focus is on the 'reasonable person' and whether a learner or trainee is expected to reach the standard of a competent hairdresser. In **Nettleship v Weston**, the court decided that a learner driver had to reach the standard of a competent driver and this could be the case here. Also a professional is judged by the standards of others in that profession as decided in **Bolam v Friern HMC** in relation to doctors and we could say a reasonable hairdresser would not make such a mistake.*

Doctor Patel made an error of judgment and the patient suffered a stroke.

The company spent a lot of money installing safety measures but Bob the boiler-man was injured when an electrical fault occurred.

When responding to an emergency call with its siren blaring, the ambulance crashed into a car, seriously injuring the driver.

In all problem questions, you need to take a logical approach. First, read the facts carefully to ensure that you understand the points raised by the scenario. Then apply the relevant law in a logical manner, using cases in support.

Examination tip

It is **good practice** to be selective. Select only the law that applies to the given facts. This shows that you understand the law well enough to know what is relevant.

It is **bad practice** to write all you know about an area just because you know it well. Even if it is right, you will gain no marks if it is not relevant to the facts given.

Task 22: Application practice – clue-spotting

As with the last exercise it is useful to practise 'clue-spotting', so here are a few more phrases from examination scenarios. Make a note any particular issues that they bring to mind, with a relevant case. The area of law is indicated in brackets and the first is done for you in italics. Again these are merely 'snippets' but in each case you can assume someone has suffered harm.

Amy was babysitting for her neighbour's three-year-old son Sergei when she falls asleep (duty and breach). *This indicates proximity is the focus regarding duty. There is a relationship between a babysitter and the child being looked after as in **Donoghue v Stevenson**, where there was a relationship between a manufacturer and consumers because a consumer is someone likely to be affected by a manufacturer's actions. Here a child is likely to be affected by a babysitter's actions. As for breach, it can be said that as Sergei is* *only three then the standard expected of Amy is higher. This is supported by **Paris v Stepney BC**, where a higher standard of care was expected because the employee was vulnerable as he was already blind in one eye so the outcome was likely to be more serious. It can also be said that a reasonable babysitter would not fall asleep while looking after a young child.*

She heard the crash and ran to the scene (duty).

He wasn't wearing a hard hat while working on scaffolding on the building site (breach).

Surprisingly it collapsed (breach and causation).

The police did not catch the man and a member of the public was assaulted (duty).

The police took the man into custody and he assaulted another prisoner (duty).

The children were playing a rough game and one was injured (breach).

Finally, make sure you cover the whole question. There are only a certain number of marks available. The examiner has a mark scheme to work to, so however brilliant your answer to one part of the question is, missing out the other parts will severely reduce your total marks.

Examination tip

Read the question carefully as sometimes you are asked to **explain** the law and sometimes to **apply** it. You can only earn marks for what you are asked to do.

Here is an examination scenario followed by some questions. These are of the type and number that you can expect, including something on the courts and / or damages. As tort is the second scenario on AQA papers (after criminal law), I have numbered the questions as you would expect to see them, starting at 07.

Task 23 Examination question

Mikaela is looking after Amir, aged 5. She leaves him playing in the garden while she goes to make a cup of coffee. He finds some slug pellets in a garden shed and eats several, thinking they are sweets. He is taken to hospital where the doctors pump his stomach and fortunately no lasting harm is done, although he is kept in for a few days for observation. His parents want to bring a personal injuries claim on his behalf for £4,000, which their solicitor tells them will be a straightforward claim.

07 Explain how the law decides whether a duty of care is owed in a negligence case. *8 marks*

08 Explain how the law decides a duty of care has been breached and explain two of the risk factors which may be taken into account. *8 marks*

Refer to the scenario when answering the remaining questions in this section.

09 Assuming Mikaela owes Amir a duty of care, discuss whether she has breached that duty. *8 marks + 2 marks for AO3*

10 Assuming duty, breach and causation in fact all apply, briefly outline the rules on remoteness of damage and discuss whether Amir's harm is too remote. *8 marks*

11 Outline the three-track case management system used in the civil cases and briefly explain which track and which court would be used in this claim against Mikaela. *5 marks*

12 Assuming that Mikaela is found to be liable in negligence explain how the court would calculate an award of damages to Amir. *8 marks*

Task 1

You may have put it slightly differently but one way of putting it would be that you should take care not to do something, or fail to do something, that might harm others. This does not mean everyone but those who are likely to be affected by your actions, e.g., people you should have considered before acting or omitting to act. Applying this to **Donoghue v Stevenson**, a manufacturer should owe a duty to a consumer because a consumer is someone likely to be affected by the actions and omissions of a manufacturer. A consumer is also someone whom a manufacturer ought to have in mind when manufacturing the product, in this case ginger beer.

Task 2

Mrs D couldn't sue the shopkeeper because she had no contract with the shopkeeper, her friend bought the drink.

She sued the manufacturer and the HL decided that a manufacturer owes a duty to the consumer.

The **Donoghue v Stevenson** case is important for establishing liability in negligence.

The neighbour principle is that a person owes a duty to someone affected by their actions.

Task 3

Applying the other two parts of the test to **Watson v British Boxing Board** it can be said that it is foreseeable that a boxer could be harmed by decisions of the Boxing Board, in particular not to provide medical assistance at the ringside. There is also proximity between the parties as there is a clear relationship between the Board and boxers, who are likely to be affected by their actions. In **Vowles v Evans**, it is foreseeable that players could be harmed by a referee's actions and again there is a clear relationship between players of any game and a referee as the players will be affected by the referee's decisions.

Task 4

Proving a duty of care is based on the neighbour principle from **Donoghue v Stevenson**, that a person owes a duty to someone affected by their actions, and the later three-part test from **Caparo v Dickman**. This says that a person owes a duty where harm is foreseeable, there is proximity between the parties (in time, space and / or relationship) and it is fair, just and reasonable to impose a duty. It is foreseeable that both a passenger and a pedestrian will be affected by a driver's actions and it is also foreseeable that either could come to harm, as was the case in **Kent v Griffiths** where the CA said a patient was owed a duty by the ambulance service because it was foreseeable that harm could occur. There is clear proximity between a driver and a passenger, not only in relationship but in space, as the passenger is in the car. There is also a relationship between a driver and other road users, whether drivers or pedestrians, again in relationship and space. Although there was not found to be sufficient proximity in **Bourhill v Young**, this was because the pedestrian was not anywhere near the scene, which is not the case here. As regards whether it is fair, just and reasonable to impose a duty, there appear to be no policy reasons to exclude one, unlike in **Hill v CC of West Yorkshire** where the police were held to be immune from owing a duty as it could make policing inefficient. The duty to the passenger is clear because there is no danger of opening the floodgates to other claims; the duty would only be to the very limited number of passengers in a car. As regards the child, although a member of the public, as in **Hill**, there is still no danger of opening the floodgates because it would again only be a duty to the limited number of people a driver encounters on the road. In conclusion Franny will owe both the passenger and the child a duty of care.

Task 5

Lord Denning meant that the court will not use hindsight to assess whether a risk is foreseeable. It is whether the risk of harm was foreseeable *at the time* of the alleged negligence. He said this in **Roe v Ministry of Health** and it is most relevant to the degree of risk: how likely something is to happen.

Self-test questions on duty

The three-part **Caparo** test is:

> there must be foreseeability of harm
>
> there must be proximity between C and D
>
> it must be fair, just and reasonable to impose a duty on D

No duty was owed in **Bourhill v Young** because there was no proximity between her and the driver as she was not at the scene.

No duty was owed in **Caparo v Dickman** because there was no proximity between the investor and the auditors, nor was it fair, just and reasonable to impose a duty.

Among others, police, hospitals, rescue services and local councils might be immune from owing a duty.

No duty was owed in **Fernquest v Swansea CC** because it was a normal hazard which people would be aware of, so it was not fair, just and reasonable to impose a duty of care. In **Vernon Knight Associates v Cornwall CC**, there was a duty because the council knew of the problem so it was much more foreseeable and therefore fairer that a duty should be imposed.

Task 6

Using **Bolton v Stone** we know that the court decided the degree of risk was low and not very foreseeable as it had rarely happened before. The potential harm could be serious though, as cricket balls are very hard and could kill. However, this is balanced against all the other factors; including not only the low degree of risk but also the precautions the cricket club had taken (erecting a high fence). It is also arguable that it was justifiable due to the social benefit of the game of cricket. On balancing these factors against each other it would seem that the club had done all that a reasonable club would do in the circumstances.

Task 7

Bolton v Stone – the cricket club owed a duty to passers-by

Paris v Stepney – the employer owed a duty to the employee

Watt v Hertfordshire CC – the council (or employer) owed a duty to the employee

Latimer v AEC – the employer owed a duty to the employee

Nettleship v Weston – the learner driver owed a duty to her driving instructor

Mullin v Richards school – pupils owed a duty to each other

Bolam v Friern HMC – the doctor owed a duty to the patient

McDonnell v Holwerda – the doctor (or general practitioner) owed a duty to the patient

Vowles v Evans – the referee owed a duty to the players

Task 8

You may have chosen others cases, but here is one example. In **The Scout Association v Mark Barnes 2010**, the important factor was whether the activity had sufficient social value to be justified. The CA thought the value was limited and therefore the risk was not justified. Applying the other factors, it can be said that the risk of harm was foreseeable because the main lights were off and the scouts were running around in the semi-dark. The seriousness of harm would not seem that great though, because there is only a limited amount of harm that can be caused by people running around indoors. The club had taken some precautions by using the emergency lighting but arguably should have removed the furniture, at least at floor level. On balance, although the gravity of the potential harm was low the other factors would come down on the side of breach. The risk was foreseeable, only minimum precautions were taken, and the lack of social value would be a deciding factor in finding the Scout Association had breached its duty.

Task 9

Here is a simple diagram with some cases added.

> ## The standard of care expected is that of the reasonable person in these circumstances:

- Reasonable parent (**Harris v Perry**)
- Reasonable employer (**Daw v Intel**)
- Reasonable child (**Mullins/Orchard v Lee**)
- Reasonable doctor (**Bolam/Bolitho**)

> ## The standard expected is based on 4 factors:

- The degree of risk (**Bolton v Stone**)
- The seriousness of potential harm (**Paris v Stepney BC**)
- Whether the risk was justifiable (**Watts**)
- The expense and practicality of taking precautions (**Latimer**)

Self-test questions on breach

The objective standard was explained by Baron Alderson in **Blyth v Birmingham Waterworks Co. 1856**

The standard expected of a professional is the standard of a person in that line of work

The standard expected of a child is the standard of a child of similar age, not an adult

The employers had breached their duty in **Daw v Intel Corp (UK) Ltd** because they already knew the employee had work-related problems. The injury was therefore foreseeable.

Task 10

The answer depends on your chosen case but here is an example. In **Paris v Stepney BC 1951**, a worker was injured in the eye whilst doing some welding. The council was found to have breached its duty because it had failed to provide goggles. It can be said that 'but for' the failure to provide goggles the worker would not have been harmed, therefore the failure caused the harm.

Task 11

The answer again depends on your chosen cases but here is one example from the duty cases and one from breach.

In **Watson v British Boxing Board 2000**, the boxer Michael Watson suffered head injuries during a fight against Chris Eubank. He sued the Board on the basis that had proper medical treatment been given at the ringside he would not have suffered brain damage. It can be said that 'but for' the failure to provide medical treatment he would not have suffered brain damage. As regards remoteness of damage, it is foreseeable that if medical treatment is not available at a boxing match where people are hitting each other, then someone could suffer harm. As harm is foreseeable it is not too remote from the negligent act or omission (the failure to provide medical treatment) so **The Wagon Mound** test is also satisfied.

In **Palmer v Cornwall CC 2009**, a boy of 14 hit another boy in the eye while throwing stones at seagulls. The CA held that only one supervisor for around 300 children was clearly inadequate so the council was in breach of duty. It can be said that 'but for' this breach the boy would not have been injured. It is also foreseeable that if there is not adequate supervision the boys may do something like this (based on the idea that children are likely to "do the unexpected" as held in **Jolley**). The harm was therefore not too remote from the breach of duty (the failure to provide adequate supervision).

Task 12

Duty: Applying the **Caparo** test to the facts of **Barnett v Kensington & Chelsea HMC**, the doctor owed a duty because it is foreseeable that a hospital's actions could cause harm to patients coming to casualty. There is a relationship between a hospital doctor and an outpatient so there is sufficient proximity. Although the hospital is a public authority (and so arguably there are policy reasons not to impose a duty), in these circumstances it is most likely to be fair, just and reasonable to impose a duty of care as a hospital should care for those who are ill. There is no 'floodgates' issue because the duty is limited to patients and not the public in general (thus it is more likely **Reeves v MPC** will be followed, rather than **Hill**).

Breach: The doctor breached his duty as he has not reached the standard of a reasonable doctor. A doctor is judged against those in the same profession so if medical opinion shows it would be more usual at least to examine the patient there will be a breach (**Bolam v Friern HMC**). This medical opinion must have some logical basis (**Bolitho v City & Hackney HA**) but that would seem to be the case as it is normal to examine patients. The courts balance several factors in deciding what is reasonable. These include how big the risk is, what harm might occur from taking the risk, whether the risk is justified and how practical it would be to avoid the risk. There is quite a high risk of harm because no examination at all took place so, in these circumstances, harm is foreseeable. The potential harm is relatively serious as he could have had any number of serious ailments which might have been picked up in an examination. There could be a public benefit in not using up valuable resources but this is unlikely to be persuasive as it is minimal in relation to the other factors. Where the risk of harm is high, there is a greater obligation to take sufficient precautions to avoid it. Here this would only require minimal precautions, just doing the examination, so it is not impractical to expect more care to be taken. In **Barnett**, on balance, the doctor did not act as a reasonable doctor would have done.

Causation: The doctor owed a duty which he breached, so the remaining issue is whether the breach caused the man's death. Causation has to be proved BOTH in fact and in law. Here causation in fact is not proved because the harm would have occurred anyway. The answer to the question 'but for the breach of duty would he have died?' is 'yes', the evidence showed that he would have died anyway, so the doctor's breach did not cause the death. As causation in fact is not proved there is no need to consider causation in law.

Self-test questions on causation
The 'but for' test asks 'but for D's action would harm have occurred?' It comes from **Barnett v Chelsea & Kensington HMC**

The Wagon Mound case established the rule on foreseeability

Hughes added that if the *type* of harm is foreseeable this is enough; the exact harm need not be

The 'thin skull rule' means that if a person is harmed because he / she is particularly vulnerable (e.g., has a thin skull), D is liable for the full consequences even if someone without the vulnerability would not have been harmed to the same degree.

The point made in **Jolley** (in the HL) in regard to children, was that they do the unexpected

Task 13
There is no answer to this task but hopefully you found some information about taking a civil case to court as well as on the alternatives and made a few notes.

Task 14
The burden of proof refers to the fact that it is on the claimant to provide evidence to prove their case, i.e., C must prove D was negligent.

The standard of proof refers to how much evidence is needed. In the tort of negligence it is enough that C provides evidence of more than a 50% chance that D was negligent.

Res ipsa loquitur means the thing speaks for itself and it has the effect of reducing the burden on C. If the rule applies then C does not have to prove D has been negligent, only that the thing that caused the harm was under D's control.

Self-test questions on the courts and damages
A small claim is one that is under £10,000 (or £1,000 in personal injury cases)

A small claim is heard in the county court

The maximum sum under the fast-track system is £25,000

A fast-track case might be transferred to the High Court if it is complex

The difference between special and general damages is that the first is quantifiable but the second has to be assessed by the court

Pecuniary loss means a financial loss. It is quantifiable in monetary terms

Task 15

In **Reeves v MPC**, the police knew the prisoner was a suicide risk so it was foreseeable harm could occur. There was only a limited number of possible claimants therefore it was also fair just and reasonable to impose a duty. On balance, a duty of care was owed to him. In **Orange v CC of West Yorkshire Police**, the claim failed because the man who hanged himself whilst in custody was *not* a known suicide risk so the harm was not foreseeable and it would not be fair in such circumstances to impose a duty so no duty was owed.

Task 16

I hope you noticed the word 'other' and did not repeat the above answer. Another two examples are **Watson v British Boxing Board 2000**, where the Board owed a duty to the boxer Michael Watson who suffered head injuries during a fight against Chris Eubank. The CA found that it was 'fair, just and reasonable' to impose a duty on the Board to ensure adequate medical facilities were available. This differed from the case of **Fernquest v Swansea CC 2011** where, although there was proximity between the council who ran the bus service and their customers, and the risk of injury was foreseeable, it was not fair, just and reasonable to impose a duty of care on a council for 'normal hazards' which members of the public could be expected to be aware of.

Task 17

The **Caparo** test for owing a duty of care is whether harm is foreseeable, whether the parties are in proximity to each other and whether it is fair, just and reasonable to impose a duty.

In **Donoghue v Stevenson**, it was foreseeable that the manufacturer's actions could harm a consumer of the ginger beer. In this case it is foreseeable that the actions of the police officer in leaving the bridge unattended would cause harm, as it was in a dangerous state.

In **Kent v Griffiths**, an ambulance service was held to be in sufficiently close proximity to a patient once it had accepted the call and sent an ambulance to collect that patient. Here the police officer had a proximate relationship with motorists near the bridge as he had taken charge of the situation.

It is fair, just and reasonable to impose a duty in these circumstances because it will not open the floodgates to claims as only a limited number of people will be in the area. It will not make policing ineffective as was the case in **Hill v CC for West Yorkshire** where it was not in the public interest to impose a duty because it could lead to defensive policing. The situation is more like **Reeves v MPC** where the police owed a duty because it would only be to a limited group of people, those in police care. The police officer will therefore owe a duty of care to the motorist who was injured.

As regards breach, this is based on what a reasonable person would do (**Blyth v Birmingham Waterworks Co.**). Firstly the courts will consider whether the police officer had acted in the way a reasonable police officer should. To assist with this several factors are balanced against each other. These are the magnitude of risk, the gravity of the potential harm, whether the risk was justifiable and the expense and practicality of taking precautions.

Here the magnitude or degree of risk was quite high because the bridge was in a dangerous state. This means harm was foreseeable, unlike in **Fardon v Harcourt-Rivington**. This factor raises the standard expected so if the risk of harm is high, greater care should be taken to avoid it. In **Bolton v Stone**, the risk was quite low so sufficient care was taken by erecting a fence. Here there was a higher risk of harm, and even if it wasn't very high, the police officer had not taken any care at all as he left it unattended. The gravity of harm is also high, as it was in **Paris v Stepney BC**, and this again raises the standard expected. A collapsing bridge could potentially cause serious harm to drivers or pedestrians nearby. There appears to be no justification for taking the risk and no social utility in his actions. This could have been the case, e.g., if he was called to an emergency in which event the standard expected is lower and he could rely on **Watt v Hertfordshire CC**, where a fire service was not in breach because they were rushing to an emergency. Finally, the police officer did not take precautions against the risk. This would not have been either expensive or impractical, as he could have done something like putting up cones, barriers or other warning signs. In both **Bolton v Stone** and **Latimer v AEC**, sufficient precautions were taken, but this is not the case here.

Balancing these factors, he did not reach the standard expected of a reasonable police officer so was in breach of duty.

Task 18

Applying the causation rules to **Gibson** we can say that 'but for' the police officer's act of leaving the scene unattended the motorist would not have been injured because he would have been warned of the danger, unlike in **Barnett** where the man would have died anyway even if the hospital had not been in breach of duty. The harm is not too remote from the breach of duty (as required by the **Wagon Mound**) because it is foreseeable that leaving a bridge in a dangerous state with no warnings could lead to someone being injured. In the **Wagon Mound**, it was foreseeable that the spilt oil could cause damage but not that it could catch fire, so the former damage could be claimed but not the damage caused by the fire, because this was too remote. Here the harm to the motorist was foreseeable so causation is proved both in fact and in law.

Task 19

The small claims track is for claims up to £10,000, or £1,000 in personal injury cases. These cases are heard by a district judge in private in a special room in the county court, usually without a solicitor.

The fast track covers claims between £10,000 and £25,000. These cases start in the county court with a district judge, who provides a strict time-table and sets limits on the costs.

The multi-track covers cases over £25,000 and these cases start in the High Court. Again the judge will manage the case and set a time-table, sometimes following a case management meeting.

Although cases on the fast track and multi-track start as described above, they may be moved up a track if very complex or down a track if simple.

Task 20

The purpose of damages is to compensate Dave and Pam not to punish Tariq. The court will attempt to put Dave and Pam in the position they would have been in had the incident not happened. For Pam, this means compensating her for the repairs to the car and any relevant expenses, e.g., paying for alternative transport while it is being repaired. The court will not need to work this out as Pam will have receipts and will include these amounts in her claim. All expenses up to the date of the trial are special damages and also pecuniary as they are quantifiable in monetary terms. This case will quite possibly be dealt with by negotiation between the parties as it is for a minor amount which is quite clear. However, if it does go to court it will be heard as a small claim in the county court.

In Dave's case there will be both special and general damages. The loss of earnings up to the trial will be quantifiable so special damages, as will be the damage to the bike and any related expenses. These are also pecuniary as explained above. As he is likely to be back at work before the trial there will be no loss of future earnings to calculate. However, the court will need to assess an amount for the injury itself using guidelines from the Judicial Studies Board. If Dave is suffering pain or distress then an award for pain and suffering may also be assessed by the court. The fact that Dave's bike is in the car may indicate that cycling is a hobby of his and if so the court may make an award for loss of amenity. This award recognises that someone may have suffered more than usual because the injury has affected something special, like a hobby. These amounts will be classed as non-pecuniary because they are not quantifiable in monetary terms.

As Dave is likely to be back at work within a matter of months, any award is likely to be by way of a lump sum. This is because structured settlements are usually only applied in cases of long-term illness or high pay-outs. If the claim is under £25,000 it will be allocated to the fast-track and is likely to be heard in the county court unless it is complex, and there is no indication of this. Although it may be under £10,000 it will not be a small claim as in cases of personal injury the limit remains at £1,000 and the scenario says he will be off work for 'several months' so his claim will be higher than £1,000.

Task 21

The doctor made an error of judgment and the patient suffered a stroke: *This is similar to the example but specific to the medical profession. It indicates that the focus is the standard of care required of the medical profession. The **Bolam** test needs to be applied in such cases, as amended by **Bolitho**. Thus Dr Patel must act in accordance with what would be normal practice in the opinion of a reasonable medical body, and that opinion must have a logical basis.*

The company spent a lot of money installing state-of-the-art safety measures but Bob the boiler-man was injured when an electrical fault occurred: *This indicates the focus is on the breach factors, in particular whether precautions against a risk have been taken and whether expecting any more would be impractical, as in **Latimer v AEC**. It seems a lot has been done as the company spent 'a lot of money' and although spending money would not usually be enough alone, it would seem sufficient precautions have been taken as the safety measures are said to be 'state-of-the-art'.*

When responding to an emergency call with its siren blaring, the ambulance crashed into a car, seriously injuring the driver: *This indicates that the breach factors are again the focus, here in particular whether the risk was justifiable. As the ambulance was reacting to an emergency this is likely to be the case, as in **Watt v Hertfordshire CC**. Also they had the 'siren blaring' so have taken precautions against the risk of harm.*

Task 22: Application practice

She heard the crash and ran to the scene (duty)

The focus here is on whether the parties were in proximity to each other. A driver would have a legal relationship with other road users including pedestrians, in the same way a manufacturer and consumer have a legal relationship as identified in **Donoghue v Stevenson**, because a consumer is likely to be affected by a manufacturer's actions. However, this would not apply to someone who was out of sight of the accident as a person on another street is not likely to be affected by a motorist's actions. It is like **Bourhill v Young** where a woman miscarried but the court held the negligent driver did not owe her a duty because she was not at the scene of the crash and had no relationship with the driver. Also in **Caparo v Dickman**, the relationship between the auditors and the company was close enough but there was insufficient proximity between the auditors and that company's potential shareholders.

He wasn't wearing a hard hat while working on scaffolding on the building site (breach).

This is based on **Paris v Stepney BC** and the focus is on the magnitude of likely harm. As he was on scaffolding he was probably working at a height and so any potential injury would be quite serious; he could even die if he fell. This means he would be owed a higher duty of care by his employers or the site manager. It leads on to the fact that if the harm might be serious then greater precautions should be taken to avoid it. He should have been told to wear a hard hat. In **Uren v Corporate Leisure**, the court held that the precaution of banning diving head-first should have been taken because this would be easy to do and would reduce the risk of harm. Similarly, it would be easy to ensure workers wear proper protective clothes to help avoid harm. Providing a hard hat is easy and although making sure it is worn may not be quite so easy it would not be impractical in the way that closing the factory would have been in **Latimer v AEC**.

Surprisingly it collapsed (breach and causation)

The focus here is on foreseeability which is a requirement of both breach and causation. With breach it is one of the factors taken into account when deciding what a reasonable person would have done. The word 'surprisingly' suggests that whatever happened was not foreseeable, as in **Fardon v Harcourt-Rivington** where the court held the dog jumping and breaking the window was not foreseeable so the owner was not in breach when a passer-by was injured.

As regards causation, the harm must be foreseeable, even if not the exact harm, at least the type of harm must be foreseeable. This was stated in **Hughes v Lord Advocate** where burns were foreseeable so the boy could claim even though the way it happened and the more extensive harm he suffered were not foreseeable. If the harm is not foreseeable it is seen as too remote and the claim will fail. This comes from the **Wagon Mound** where a ship had spilt oil and it caused both oil damage and a fire. It was not known that the oil could catch fire so the damage by fire was not foreseeable. It was therefore too remote from the breach of duty of spilling the oil, and only the damage done by the oil itself could be claimed. The word 'surprisingly' suggests that any resulting harm would not be foreseeable in the same way that the fire damage was not foreseeable in the **Wagon Mound**. It can be said that because it was unknown that the oil could catch fire, the fire damage was 'surprising' and based on this the damage cause by whatever 'surprisingly' collapsed would be too remote.

The police did not catch the man and a member of the public was assaulted (duty)

The focus here is on the third part of the **Caparo** test, that it must be fair, just and reasonable to impose a duty. This is a matter of public policy and means that the court looks at what is best for society as a whole. The court may restrict the duty to avoid 'opening the floodgates' to claims or because D is a public body or performing a public service. This is shown in **Hill v CC for West Yorkshire** in very similar circumstances where a man was released from police custody and he went on to kill someone. No duty was owed to the victim because to impose a duty in these circumstances could lead to less effective policing. Here there is even less likely to be a duty because not only will the same point apply but also there is less proximity as well because this time the man was never in police custody.

The police took the man into custody and he assaulted another prisoner (duty)

The focus here is again on the third part of the **Caparo** test as described above. That it must be fair, just and reasonable to impose a duty overlaps with the other two parts of the test, foreseeability and proximity. The more foreseeable something is and the more proximate the relationship, then the more likely it is that the court will find it fair, just and reasonable to impose a duty. There is a high level of proximity here because the man is in custody and so is the other prisoner. As regards foreseeability, much will depend on what the police know about the man. If the police know the man is violent it is likely that a duty will be imposed as harm is then foreseeable, as was the case in **Reeves v MPC** where a man was known to be a suicide risk so the police owed him a duty. However, if the man is not known to be violent then the case of **Orange v CC of West Yorkshire Police** is more likely to be followed because the harm will not be foreseeable. In **Orange**, the police did not owe a duty to a prisoner who committed suicide because it was not known that he was a suicide risk.

The children were playing a rough game and one was injured (breach)

Here the focus is on what a reasonable person would do, which is the test for establishing a breach of duty as stated in **Blyth v Birmingham Waterworks Co.** . This is an objective test so based not on what D sees as the correct thing to do, but on what a normal person would do in the same circumstances as D. The test changes slightly for children however, as stated in **Mullins v Richards**. In that case a schoolgirl of 15 was injured during a play-fight with another girl, so the facts are similar to these. The CA found the other girl not to be liable in negligence because a child is less likely to recognise the risks involved in rough or lively games, even though an adult may have seen such a risk. This is likely to be the case here too.

Task 23: Answer to examination practice with examiner comments (in italics)
07 When deciding whether a duty of care is owed in a negligence case the courts will consider the neighbour test from Donoghue v Stevenson along with the three-part test from Caparo v Dickman. The neighbour test is that you owe a duty to people likely to be closely and directly affected by your actions. This is based on foreseeability of harm along with proximity between the claimant (C) and defendant (D) and is similar to the first two parts of the Caparo test. The law will only impose a duty if the risk of harm is foreseeable, as in Kent v Griffiths where it was foreseeable that a delay in an ambulance arriving could risk further harm to C. As regards proximity this can be in time, space or relationship. An example is

Bourhill v Young where none of these was satisfied because the woman was not at the scene (space) did not see the event immediately (time) and had no relationship to the driver. If she had been nearby there would have been a relationship as road users would owe a duty to each other and pedestrians are people likely to be affected by a driver's actions.

The third part of the test was added in the Caparo case and relates to policy. The court will consider whether it is fair, just and reasonable to impose a duty, i.e., is it in the public interest? There are two main issues relating to policy, one is where D is carrying out a public service so that imposing a duty may detract from this and not been seen as fair. This occurred in Hill where the police did not owe a duty to a victim of Jack the Ripper because making the police owe a duty to every unknown member of the public could lead to them being too defensive and less efficient. This could also apply to councils and hospitals which also carry out public services. The other part to whether it is fair, just and reasonable to impose a duty is called the 'floodgates' issue. This is where the court will consider whether imposing a duty would lead to a flood of other claims. An example is Caparo itself because if the auditors owed a duty to anyone who saw the accounts there could be millions of claims as company accounts are public.

Examiner comment
This is a comprehensive answer with clear explanations and case examples for each part of the test for imposing a duty of care. The full 8 marks would be awarded. (There would be no loss of marks for the slight confusion between Jack the ripper and the Yorkshire ripper as this does not in any way detract from the explanation).

08 There are four risk factors which may be taken into account in deciding if a duty is breached. These are the degree of risk, the gravity of the potential harm, whether the risk was justifiable and the expense and practicality of taking precautions. In Bolton v Stone the cricket club had put up a high fence and a ball had hardly ever gone over it so the risk was low. This meant the cricket club had not breached their duty to a woman passing by who was hit by a ball. In Paris v Stepney the likely harm was high as the man doing some welding was blind in one eye already so if he was hurt in the other eye it would be that much more serious so his employer should have made him wear goggles. This time the duty was breached. In Latimer v AEC a factory would have had to shut down after a flood to avoid the risk of anyone slipping and getting injured, which wasn't practical. In Watt v Hertfordshire the fire service was going to a car accident so taking the risk of carrying the jack on an unsuitable lorry was justifiable. In both these cases there was no breach of duty.

Examiner comment
*This is clearly a pre-prepared answer to a question on the risk factors, which is a shame given the candidate's obvious ability as shown in question 07. There is no explanation of the reasonable person, i.e., that it is an objective test (**Blyth** and **Nettleship**)) but that the standard is lower for children (**Mullins**) and higher for professionals (**Bolam/Bolitho**). Also all four factors are discussed when only two were needed. Not only does this mean that two explanations are wasted as marks cannot be given for material that was not requested, but also that the candidate did not have time to explain the effect of the factors on the standard expected, i.e., how the standard expected of the reasonable person may be raised (if the risk is high, the victim is vulnerable and / or precautions are easy) or lowered (if the risk is low, precautions would be impractical and / or the risk is justified). It is unlikely that more than*

half marks would be awarded. Candidates should be aware of the importance of answering the question set and not the one they had hoped for.

09 Mikaela will be compared to a reasonable person looking after a young child. It does not say how old Mikaela is or whether she is a professional carer. A professional person is compared to others in that profession when deciding if an act is reasonable, as decided in Bolam. It is unlikely that a reasonable carer would leave a young child alone. Even if she is a trainee or inexperienced carer she will be expected to reach the standard of a reasonably competent one as for the learner driver in Nettleship v Weston. She is therefore likely to be in breach of duty but the court will take into account several factors when deciding this. In Paris v Stepney, discussed above, the standard expected was higher because the man was particularly vulnerable. This could be the same for a child so Mikaela should take greater care. Other factors are the degree of risk and taking precautions. The reasonable person is not expected to take care against minute risks but where the risk of harm is high more is expected and children can be easily hurt. Mikaela would therefore be expected to take precautions. Unlike in Latimer, discussed above, these would be neither costly nor impractical. In Uren v Corporate Leisure 2013 the court said precautions should have been taken against the risk of harm from diving head first into a shallow pool because it would be easy just to ban diving in head first. All Mikaela has to do is take Amir with her when she goes to make coffee so it is more likely that Uren will be followed than Latimer. I think Mikaela will be found in breach of her duty of care to Amir because she has not taken enough precautions and has not acted as a reasonable person would.

Examiner comment

This is an excellent response, this time with both the reasonable person and the risk factors clearly explained and applied, with appropriate and relevant cases. The answer is directed at the particular facts of the scenario, and has a conclusion based on the application. Reference to explanations given earlier is quite acceptable as long as the law is applied to the specific facts. Although the standard cases on the factors are perfectly valid examples it is refreshing to see a newer case used to help explain how the law applies by providing a comparison. Full marks for both the answer and AO3 would be awarded (10 marks in total) as the law is expressed clearly with very few errors of grammar.

10 The rules on remoteness of damage come from the Wagon Mound. A ship had spilt oil and it caused oil damage and also a fire which damaged a wharf. The oil should not normally have caught fire and it was not even known that it could do. This meant the damage by fire was not foreseeable so it was too remote from the breach of duty which was spilling the oil so it did not legally cause the harm. A good case to show how the law looks at remoteness in the case of children is Jolley v Sutton. The court said that children could be expected to do the unexpected. This means it is likely to be seen as foreseeable that Amir could come to harm if left in a garden with a shed in it as there are often all sorts of poisons in a shed such as weedkillers and pesticides. Also the 'but for' test which is also used in causation will apply. This comes from the medical case of Barnett and asks whether Amir would have been harmed but for Mikaela's negligence and we can so 'no' to this because if she had taken him with her he would not have found the slug pellets.

Examiner comment

Although quite brief this answer deals with the main point raised by the question fairly adequately, and uses an appropriate case in support. The candidate discusses the 'but for' test which is not needed but would not lose marks (though it costs precious time so this type of mistake should be avoided). For the higher mark band however, reference should be made to **Hughes v Lord Advocate** to explain that if the type of harm is foreseeable, then the fact that it occurred in an unforeseeable way, or that the consequences were more extensive than could be foreseen, will not affect liability. The exact harm (swallowing slug pellets and having to have his stomach pumped) does not therefore have to be foreseeable as long as some harm is, and it is foreseeable that a child might be inquisitive and thereby suffer some kind of harm. The thin-skull rule should also be mentioned briefly, to explain that even if Amir is particularly vulnerable, as young children often are, Mikaela will be liable for the full consequences of her breach as stated in **Smith v Leech-Brain**.

11 There are three different tracks for civil cases. The first track is the small claims track in the county court. The maximum claim for this track is £10,000, and in personal injury cases it is £1,000. The next track is the fast track and this deals with claims between £10,000 and £25,000. Cases on this track will also start in the county court. The third track is the multi-track and all cases over £25,000 are allocated to this track and start in the High Court. The judge will manage the case and set a time-table so time and costs are kept low. Sometimes a fast track case may be transferred to the High court if it is complex. Similarly a simple case may be heard in the county court even though the amount of money means it starts in the High Court.

In this claim against Mikaela the claim is likely to be on the fast track in the county court because the solicitor says it is simple but it is over the £1,000 limit for a small claim for personal injury.

12 The court would calculate an award of damages by dividing the claim into special and general damages. Special damages are those before the trial. General damages must be assessed by the court and these are for the injury itself plus loss of amenity and pain and suffering. There are also pecuniary and non-pecuniary damages. The first are financial losses, things that can be set down as an amount of money. Non-pecuniary losses are not quantifiable in this way and the court assesses them. Sometimes a structured settlement is given and the money is paid in instalments but this is usually for big claims.

Overall this is a strong answer but would probably not quite reach the A grade. The failure to answer the question set in 08 and the lack of application in 12 is what let this candidate down. The rest was excellent but an examiner cannot transfer marks from one part of a question to another. A brief discussion of the reasonable person or the effect of the factors in raising or lowering the care expected would have sufficed to get this comfortably into the top grade, or alternatively a brief application to Amir's claim in the final question would have done so.

The following abbreviations are commonly used. You may use them in an examination answer, but write them in full the first time, e.g., write 'actual bodily harm (ABH)' and then after that you can just write 'ABH'.

General

Draft Code – A Criminal Code for England and Wales (Law Commission No. 177), 1989

CCRC Criminal Cases Review Commission

ABH actual bodily harm

GBH grievous bodily harm

D defendant

C claimant

V Victim

CA Court of Appeal

HL House of Lords

SC Supreme Court

Acts

S – Section (thus **s 1** Theft Act 1968 refers to section 1 of that Act)

S 1(2) means section 1 subsection 2 of an Act.

OAPA – Offences against the Person Act 1861

In cases – these don't need to be written in full

CC (at beginning) chief constable

CC (at end) county council

BC borough council

DC district council

LBC London borough council

AHA Area Health Authority

J Justice

LJ Lord Justice

LCJ Lord Chief Justice

LC Lord Chancellor

AG Attorney General

CPS Crown Prosecution Service

DPP Director of Public Prosecutions

AG Attorney General

www.ingramcontent.com/pod-product-compliance
Lightning Source LLC
Chambersburg PA
CBHW070959180526
45168CB00003B/1208